GRADE 2

Treasures

TESTED ✔

P9-AQG-829

Unit Assessment

Includes Writing Prompts

Macmillan/McGraw-Hill

PHOTOGRAPHY CREDITS
104: Pete Souza.

A

The McGraw·Hill Companies

 Macmillan/McGraw-Hill

Published by Macmillan/McGraw-Hill, of McGraw-Hill Education, a division of The McGraw-Hill Companies, Inc.,
Two Penn Plaza, New York, New York 10121.

Printed in the United States of America

1 2 3 4 5 6 7 8 9 079 13 12 11 10 09

Contents

Introduction to the Unit Assessment

The Unit Assessment is designed to measure your children's mastery of the specific skills taught in each unit of the *Treasures* reading program. The test questions use formats your children may encounter on standardized tests.

The Unit Assessments may test skills that are not evaluated on your state test but that are important skills in the *Treasures* program. Each Unit Assessment includes questions that cover the following areas:

- Listening Comprehension
- Reading Comprehension
- Vocabulary Strategies
- Literary Elements
- Text Features and Study Skills
- Grammar, Mechanics, and Usage
- Phonics
- Writing

When scheduling the Unit Assessment, you will need to decide whether to administer it in one or more sessions. You may choose to give the first section of the Unit Assessment in one sitting and schedule the writing topic for another time.

How to Use the Unit Assessment

The Unit Assessment is given at the end of each unit, after the fifth week of instruction. Each assessment includes fiction and nonfiction passages and questions focusing on the main skills taught throughout the unit. There also is a writing prompt that gives children an opportunity to practice writing in a test situation. The type of writing is the same as the one focused on in the unit.

Sample Questions are included on **pages viii–ix** of this book to familiarize children with the format of standardized test items. They should be used before the first Unit Assessment; you may choose to review them with the children again before each test. Have children follow along as you read the instructions aloud. Allow children time to read the sample passage and then go over the questions and answers with them, answering any questions.

Anchor papers are provided for the six writing prompts. These papers illustrate the kinds of responses children are likely to write, as well as the most common kinds of errors found in children's writing at this grade level. These **Anchor Papers** can be found on **pages 164–187.**

Using the Results to Inform Instruction

Use the results of the Unit Assessment as a formative assessment tool to help monitor each child's progress. Information gathered by evaluating the results of this assessment also can be used to diagnose specific strengths and weaknesses of your children. If you use Unit Assessment scores to help determine report card grades, then you can consider the tests to be summative assessments as well.

The Unit Assessment scores should be one of multiple measures used to help make instructional decisions for the coming unit. Analyze which skills children have mastered and which ones require further reteaching. This information, along with the results of other assessments and your own observations, can be used to determine grouping and instructional decisions. Another way to use the Unit Assessment results is to compare them with the results of the corresponding Selection Tests and Weekly Assessments. Determine whether changes in instruction or additional small group support improved children's scores. The **Unit Reteaching and Intervention Charts** on **pages 188–193** will help you develop your reteaching plans.

Administering the Unit Assessment

Each Unit Assessment consists of 28 multiple-choice questions and two short-answer questions. Each test also includes a writing prompt. The format of the test is the same for each unit. You may want to explain each section of the test to children the first time you administer it.

- For the multiple-choice questions, children should fill in the oval next to the answer they have chosen. (If you are using the separate Answer Sheet, direct children to fill in the circle for the answer they have chosen.) Remind children to make their marks dark and neat.

- For the short-answer questions, children should write their answers on the lines provided on the page. (If you are using the separate Answer Sheet, direct children to write their answers on the back of the Answer Sheet.)

- For the writing prompt, children should use the lined pages provided in the test booklet.

- The introductory pages that precede each Unit Assessment provide suggested scripts to follow when administering the test.

An **Answer Sheet** can be found on **page 145,** if you choose to use one.

The **Answer Keys** to score the tests can be found on **pages 148–159.**

General Procedures

Before the test: Distribute copies of the Unit Assessment and Answer Sheet, if you choose to use one.

Directions: Say: *Write your name and the date on the cover of your test booklet.* (If you are using the separate Answer Sheet, say: *Write your name and the date at the top of your Answer Sheet.*) When all children are finished, say: *Open the test booklet to page 2.*

During the test: Monitor children's test-taking behavior to make sure that each child is following the directions and writing responses in the correct places.

Answer questions about procedures and materials, but do not help children answer the test questions.

After the test: Before collecting the papers, make sure that children have written their names on the test booklet or at the top of the Answer Sheet.

© Macmillan/McGraw-Hill

Scoring the Unit Assessment

Using the Student Evaluation Charts

A Student Evaluation Chart follows each Unit Assessment. It lists all of the skills covered and the number of the question that assesses each skill.

- In the column labeled "Number Correct," fill in the point value for the questions answered correctly for each skill. Add the total number of points for correct responses and write the number for each subtest next to the total possible score.

- Add the scores for each skill (point value of the items answered correctly) to determine the total test score.

- To convert these raw test scores to percentages, divide the point value of the questions answered correctly by the total number of points. Example: A child earns 24 out of 32 possible points; 24 divided by 32 = .75 or 75%.

Multiple-choice questions are worth one point each. Short-answer questions are worth three points each. Writing prompts are worth four points.

Use the **Short-Answer Reading Rubric** on **page 147** to score the short-answer questions.

This program uses a holistic scoring system to score written compositions. Children's writing will be assessed in five domains: Focus and Coherence, Organization, Development of Ideas, Voice, and Conventions. The assigned score represents the child's command of the domains. Use the scoring criteria contained in the **Writing Rubrics** on **pages 160–163** to determine the overall level of the child's writing.

Evaluating the Scores

The primary focus of the Unit Assessments is to measure each child's progress toward mastery of each skill. Scores that fall below the 80th percentile suggest that children require additional instruction before mastery of that skill can be achieved.

Evaluating the results of these assessments provides specific information about children's daily instructional needs. We recommend that you use these results for instructional planning and reteaching opportunities. Compare these results with your own observations of children's work and identify objectives that need further reinforcement. Incorporate these objectives into your instructional plans for the upcoming unit for individual, small group, or whole group instruction as indicated.

Reading Sample

DIRECTIONS

Read "Playful Cats." Then read each question. Decide which is the best answer to each question. Mark the space for the answer you have chosen.

Playful Cats

1   Ben had a new kitten named Tiger. Ben liked to pull a string across the floor and watch Tiger chase it. Sometimes Tiger played with a toy mouse. Ben liked it when Tiger fell asleep in his lap.

2   One day Ben's friend Jane came to his house. She brought her cat, Bingo, to play with Tiger. The two cats liked to play together. They chased string. Then they ran around the room. Ben and Jane laughed at their cats. They had a lot of fun.

S-1 How are Ben and Jane alike?

(A) They have toy mice.

(B) They both like cats.

(C) Their cats fell asleep.

(D) They both like Tiger.

S-2 The story takes place —

(A) at Jane's house

(B) in the classroom

(C) at Ben's house

(D) in the playground

STOP

Revising and Editing Sample

DIRECTIONS

Read the introduction and the passage that follows. Then read each question and fill in the correct answer.

This is a story that Jan wrote. The story has mistakes. Read the story. Then answer the questions.

Sam and I

(1) We ride the bus to school every day. (2) I sit next to my friend, sam. (3) We are next door neighbors. (4) Sam and I are both in the second grade. (5) We are always excited to get to school.

S-3 What change, if any, should be made in sentence 2?

- (A) Change *I* to **i**
- (B) Change *friend* to **frend**
- (C) Change *sam* to **Sam**
- (D) Make no change

S-4 What change, if any, should be made in sentence 4?

- (A) Change *Sam and I* to **Me and Sam**
- (B) Change *second* to **seccond**
- (C) Change *both* to **Both**
- (D) Make no change

STOP

This Unit Assessment is designed to measure your children's mastery of the skills taught in the unit. The test assesses all of the following areas:

- Listening Comprehension
- Reading Comprehension
- Vocabulary Strategies
- Literary Elements
- Text Features and Study Skills
- Grammar, Mechanics, and Usage
- Phonics
- Writing

Listening Comprehension, page 2

Say: *Listen while I read this story to you. You will be asked to answer three multiple-choice questions based on this story. Listen carefully. We will begin now.*

Sam and the Balloon

Rosa and Maria were playing in the backyard with their dog, Sam. Rosa said, "Let's play the balloon game!"

"How do you play?" asked Maria.

"We'll hit a balloon in the air. We'll try to keep it away from Sam," said Rosa.

Maria blew up a big, red balloon.

First, Rosa hit the balloon to Maria. Then, Maria hit the balloon to Rosa. Rosa missed and BANG! The balloon popped right on Sam's nose. Sam's tail went between his legs. The frightened dog ran into the house.

The children went to find their pet. Maria looked under the table. Rosa looked under the beds. Mrs. Sanchez even went out to look under the car. They called and called for Sam. There was no sign of their little black dog. Finally, they gave up their hunt.

"Look what I found!" said Mr. Sanchez an hour later. There was Sam asleep in the clothes basket!

Now have children turn to page 2 and read the directions at the top of the page. Then say: *Answer questions 1–3 on page 2. Read each question carefully. To answer a question, fill in the oval next to the answer you have chosen. Mark only one oval for each question. Make your marks dark and neat. Stop when you reach the stop sign on the bottom of page 2. When you have finished, put down your pencils and look at me. You may begin now.*

Have children answer questions 1 through 3 and stop on page 2.

Reading Comprehension; Vocabulary Strategies; Literary Elements; Text Features and Study Skills; Grammar, Mechanics, and Usage, pages 3–15

Have children turn to page 3. Say: *You will now answer some multiple-choice and short-answer questions. Read all of the selections and questions carefully. You will see that the paragraphs in the reading selections and the lines in the poem are numbered. There also is a number before each sentence in the passage on page 14. These numbers will help you find the sentence or sentences you will need to* answer the questions that follow. For each multiple-choice question, read all four answer choices. To answer a multiple-choice question, fill in the oval next to the answer you have chosen. Mark only one oval for each question. Make your marks dark and neat. For each short-answer question, write your answer on the lines provided on the page. Stop when you reach the stop signs and wait for me to tell you to go on. When you have finished, put down your pencils and look at me. You may begin now.

Have children answer questions 4 through 24 and stop on page 15.

Phonics,
pages 16–17

Have children turn to page 16. Say: *I will say the name of each picture. After I say the name, read the four answer choices. Fill in the oval next to the word that names the picture. Mark your answers very carefully and make your marks dark and neat. Are there any questions?*

Respond to any questions.

Say: *Look at Number 25. I will say the name of the picture. "Pot." "Pot." Read the four answer choices and fill in the oval next to the word "Pot."*

Pause for children to mark their answers.

Say: *We will continue in the same way.*

Number 26: Rabbit

Number 27: Bed

Number 28: Face

Number 29: Fish

Number 30: Bone

Say: *Now put your pencils down and look at me.*

Writing,
pages 18–21

Have children turn to pages 18–19. Say: *Look at the writing prompt on page 18. It is followed by planning page 19. Use this blank page to plan your composition. You may want to make notes to decide what to write. You may want to make a web to put your ideas in an order that makes sense. You may want to write a rough draft. Remember that the more planning you do, the clearer your composition will be.*

Have children turn to pages 20–21. Say: *When you are ready to write your composition, be sure to write on answer document pages 20 and 21, which are the two pages with lines. Your composition does not have to completely fill these two lined pages, but it must not be longer than the two pages.*

Make sure children know what they are expected to do.

Say: *When you have finished writing, put down your pencil and look at me. You may begin writing now.*

Student Name _____

Date _____

Unit Assessment
TESTED SKILLS AND STRATEGIES

- **Listening Comprehension**
- **Reading Comprehension**
- **Vocabulary Strategies**
- **Literary Elements**
- **Text Features and Study Skills**
- **Grammar, Mechanics, and Usage**
- **Phonics**
- **Writing**

Macmillan/McGraw-Hill

DIRECTIONS

Listen as your teacher reads the selection. Then read each question. Decide which is the best answer to each question. Mark the space for the answer you have chosen.

1 Why did Sam run into the house?

(A) He wanted to play with the balloon.

(B) The balloon popped on his nose.

(C) He was hungry and wanted to eat.

(D) He wanted to sleep in the clothes basket.

2 What problem did the Sanchez family have?

(A) The balloon popped.

(B) Sam was not under the car.

(C) They could not find Sam.

(D) Rosa missed the balloon.

3 When the balloon popped on his nose, Sam felt —

(A) frightened

(B) happy

(C) angry

(D) sad

STOP

DIRECTIONS

Read each selection. Then read each question that follows that selection. Decide which is the best answer to each question. Mark the space for the answer you have chosen. Write your answers to questions 8 and 14.

Kim's Good Idea

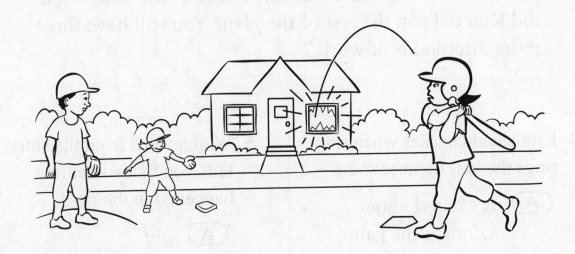

1   Kim had never hit a beautiful fly ball like this one! It sailed up and went right out of the playing field. Then came the awful sound of breaking glass. The ball had gone right through Mrs. Neal's front window!

2   "Let's get out of here!" shouted Lola as she grabbed her jacket.

3   "Wait!" said Dan. "Someone will have to talk to Mrs. Neal. She knows we always play here."

4   Kim walked slowly up to Mrs. Neal's front door. Her hand shook a little as she rang the bell. Mrs. Neal was very <u>unhappy</u>, but she was willing to talk things over. Kim said that she did not have enough money to pay for it. Kim had an idea, and Mrs. Neal liked it.

GO ON

Page 3

5   The next day, Kim and her friends were at Mrs. Neal's house. Dan and Ricky cut the grass, and Lola watered the garden. Kim and Greg washed Mrs. Neal's car. Later, Mrs. Neal came out of the house. "What a great job you've done! You are a wonderful team," she said. "And did Kim tell you the rest of the plan? You still have three more afternoons of work."

---

4 Kim's hand shakes when she rings the bell because she—

A is excited about winning the game

B hurt her hand when she hit the fly ball

C is happy to see Mrs. Neal

D is nervous about telling Mrs. Neal what happened

5 Which word from the story tells you that something happened in the past?

A *are*

B *grabbed*

C *tell*

D *knows*

© Macmillan/McGraw-Hill

GO ON ▶

6 How does Kim solve the problem of the broken window?

A She and her friends make a new window.

B She and her friends do chores for Mrs. Neal.

C She and her friends ask their parents for money.

D She and her friends don't tell anyone.

7 In paragraph 4, the word <u>unhappy</u> means —

A never happy

B more happy

C very happy

D not happy

8 What did you think Kim's good idea would be? Explain your answer and support it with details from the story.

_____

_____

_____

_____

Jungle Hunters

1   Have you ever seen a cat hunt for a mouse? Have you watched a pet cat pounce in the grass? Big cats can hunt and pounce, too! The biggest cat is a tiger. Tigers hunt for food. Tigers are great hunters.

2   You will not see this cat in your backyard. Tigers live in a forest or jungle. Tigers are found in India, Asia, and Russia. But you might see one at the zoo.

3   Tigers have striped fur. The stripes are yellow, orange, red, and black. The stripes match the long grass in the jungle. This helps the tiger camouflage, or hide by matching what is around it. Camouflage helps the tiger disappear. That helps the tiger hunt other animals.

4   Tigers stay awake at night to hunt. Then they sleep for 16 to 20 hours each day. Tigers can run very fast. They hide their claws when they run. However, they are unable to run for very long. They can move slowly and quietly to surprise their prey. They use their large, strong paws to catch it.

5   Baby tigers are called cubs. Tiger cubs cannot hunt. Their mothers have to hunt food for them. By the time they turn two, cubs learn to hunt. Now it is their turn to pounce!

© Macmillan/McGraw-Hill

9 Look at the chart.

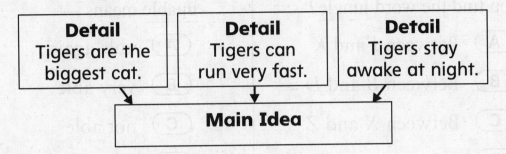

| **Detail** Tigers are the biggest cat. | **Detail** Tigers can run very fast. | **Detail** Tigers stay awake at night. |

Main Idea

Which of these goes in the *Main Idea* box?

A Tigers are furry.

B Tigers are good hunters.

C Tigers are good parents.

D Tiger cubs.

---

10 Which word from paragraph 1 shows that something happened in the past?

A *hunt*

B *watched*

C *pounce*

D *can*

11 When do tigers sleep?

A All winter

B When they turn two

C During the night

D During the day

GO ON

12 Where in the dictionary will you find the word <u>jungle</u>?

   Ⓐ Between *I* and *K*

   Ⓑ Between *B* and *D*

   Ⓒ Between *X* and *Z*

   Ⓓ Between *L* and *N*

13 In paragraph 4, the word <u>unable</u> means —

   Ⓐ able again

   Ⓑ very able

   Ⓒ not able

   Ⓓ eager

14 How do stripes help a tiger? Explain your answer and support it with details from the article.

_____

_____

_____

_____

DIRECTIONS

Read the poem. Then read each question that follows the poem. Decide which is the best answer to each question. Mark the space for the answer you have chosen.

Pedro's Puppy

1   Pedro heard his puppy's cries,
2   He saw her deep, sad, brown eyes.
3   Then she saw Pedro's small face,
4   And her tail began to race.

5   Pedro smiled, and picked her up,
6   Then she was a happy pup!

GO ON

15 Which words from the poem rhyme?

- **A** *face* and *race*
- **B** *eyes* and *tail*
- **C** *happy* and *pup*
- **D** *puppy's* and *cries*

16 How many beats are in each line?

- **A** Three
- **B** Four
- **C** Seven
- **D** Eleven

STOP

Student Name _____

DIRECTIONS
Decide which is the best answer to each question. Mark the space for the answer you have chosen.

17 Look at the picture and read the caption.

A firefighter teaching about fire safety.

The author uses the picture and caption to show —

(A) children learning about the police

(B) adults learning about fire safety

(C) how to play ball games safely

(D) children learning about fire safety

GO ON

18 Look at the title page.

Moon Beam
by
Les Kirk

Art by
Jesse Cain

Tex Publishing Company
W. Austin, Washington

What is found on this title page?

A Author's name

B Table of contents

C Index

D Glossary

GO ON ▶

Use the bar graph to answer questions 19 and 20.

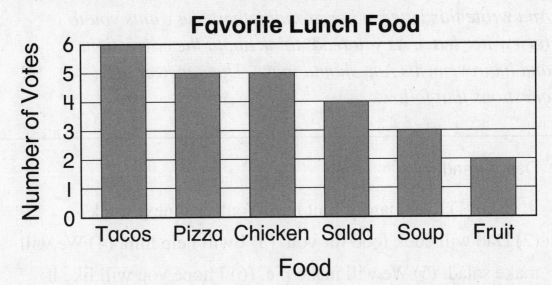

Favorite Lunch Food

19 Based on the graph, which food do the most children like best?

(A) Fruit

(B) Tacos

(C) Salad

(D) Chicken

20 Which two lunch foods are liked by the same number of children?

(A) Hot dogs and soup

(B) Tacos and pizza

(C) Chicken and pizza

(D) Soup and salad

STOP

Read the introduction and the passage that follows. Then read each question and fill in the correct answer.

Ana wrote this letter to her grandmother. She wants you to review her letter. As you read, think about the corrections and improvements Ana should make. Then answer the questions that follow.

Dear Grandma,

    (1) I can hardly wait until Your visit next week? (2) Dad will cook food for you. (3) I will help him. (4) We will make salad. (5) We will make pie. (6) I hope you will like it.

        (7) love

        (8) Ana

GO ON ▶

21 What is the **BEST** way to rewrite sentence 1?

- **A** I can hardly wait until Your visit next week
- **B** I can hardly wait until your visit next week!
- **C** I can hardly wait until Your visit next week,
- **D** I can hardly wait until your Visit next week.

22 Which word is the subject in sentence 2?

- **A** cook
- **B** Dad
- **C** food
- **D** you

23 What is the **BEST** way to combine sentences 4 and 5?

- **A** We will make salad pie.
- **B** We will make salad and pie.
- **C** We will make salad make pie.
- **D** We will make salad will make pie.

24 What is the **BEST** way to write line 7?

- **A** love,
- **B** Love.
- **C** Love,
- **D** love!

STOP

DIRECTIONS
Mark the space for the word that names the picture.

25

(A) Pot

(B) Pit

(C) Pet

(D) Potted

26

(A) Rat

(B) Rib

(C) Rabbit

(D) Ribbon

27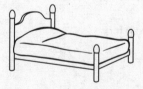

(A) Bed

(B) Bid

(C) Bud

(D) Bucket

GO ON ▶

Unit Assessment

28

(A) Fake

(B) Fan

(C) Lace

(D) Face

29

(A) Flash

(B) Fine

(C) Fish

(D) Fist

30

(A) Bin

(B) Bottom

(C) Ban

(D) Bone

Page 17

WRITTEN COMPOSITION

Write a story about a time when something happened to you on your way to school.

The information in the box below will help you remember what you should think about when you write your composition.

REMEMBER TO –

- write about something that happened to you on your way to school

- make sure that every sentence you write helps the reader understand your composition

- include enough details to help the reader clearly understand what you are saying

- use correct spelling, capitalization, punctuation, grammar, and sentences

Page 18

Student Name _____

> USE THIS PREWRITING PAGE TO
> PLAN YOUR COMPOSITION

> MAKE SURE THAT YOU WRITE YOUR COMPOSITION ON
> THE LINES ON PAGES 20-21

Page 19

Answer Document

_____

_____

_____

_____

_____

_____

_____

_____

_____

_____

Page 20

Answer Document

_____

_____

_____

_____

_____

_____

_____

_____

_____

Page 21

Grade 2 • Unit 1
Student Evaluation Chart

Tested Skills	Number Correct	Percent Correct
Listening Comprehension: *Character, 1, 3; Plot, 2*	/3	%
Reading Comprehension: *Character, 4; Plot, 6; Main Idea/ Details, 9, 11*	/4	%
Short answer: *Make/Confirm Predictions, 8; Main Idea/ Details, 14*	/6	%
Vocabulary Strategies: *Words Ending in -ed, 5, 10; Prefixes, 7, 13; Dictionary/ABC Order, 12*	/5	%
Literary Elements: *Rhyme, 15; Rhythmic Patterns, 16*	/2	%
Text Features and Study Skills: *Photos and Captions, 17; Using Parts of a Book, 18; Bar Graphs, 19, 20*	/4	%
Grammar, Mechanics, and Usage: *Sentence Capitalization and Punctuation, 21; Subjects and Predicates, 22; Sentence Combining, 23; Letter Punctuation, 24*	/4	%
Phonics: *Short o, 25; Short a, 26; Short e, 27; Soft c, 28; Consonant Digraph sh, 29; Long o, 30*	/6	%
Writing: *Personal Narrative*	/4	%
Total Unit Test Score	**/38**	**%**

This Unit Assessment is designed to measure your children's mastery of the skills taught in the unit. The test assesses all of the following areas:

- Listening Comprehension
- Reading Comprehension
- Vocabulary Strategies
- Literary Elements
- Text Features and Study Skills
- Grammar, Mechanics, and Usage
- Phonics
- Writing

Listening Comprehension, page 2

Say: *Listen while I read this story to you. You will be asked to answer three multiple-choice questions based on this story. Listen carefully. We will begin now.*

Free Pets

Sarah wanted all the children in the school to see her poster. She drew a red border on the poster and drew some pictures. This would help the children spot it. She read over what she wrote and made sure she had not made any spelling mistakes. Sarah smoothed out the poster. She found a good spot on the cafeteria bulletin board. Sarah tacked it to the board so everyone would see it.

This is what her poster said:

Rags, my pet hamster, has eight babies. And you can have one free! They are really cute and friendly. Hamsters look like mice but are larger. They are easy to care for—just feed them apples,

nuts, or carrots. You can hold your pet hamster in your hand. Surprise your mom—take one home today. Hurry, before they are all gone!

Sarah J. Room 21

Now have children turn to page 2 and read the directions at the top of the page. Then say: *Answer questions 1–3 on page 2. Read each question carefully. To answer a question, fill in the oval next to the answer you have chosen. Mark only one oval for each question. Make your marks dark and neat. Stop when you reach the stop sign on the bottom of page 2. When you have finished, put down your pencils and look at me. You may begin now.*

Have children answer questions 1 through 3 and stop on page 2.

Reading Comprehension; Vocabulary Strategies; Literary Elements; Text Features and Study Skills; Grammar, Mechanics, and Usage, pages 3–15

Have children turn to page 3. Say: *You will now answer some multiple-choice and short-answer questions. Read all of the selections and questions carefully. You will see that the paragraphs in the reading selections and the lines in the poem are numbered. There also is a number before each sentence in the passage on page 14. These numbers will help you find the sentence or sentences you will need to answer the questions that follow. For each multiple-choice question, read all four answer choices. To answer a multiple-choice question, fill in the oval next to the answer you have chosen. Mark only one oval for each question. Make your marks dark and neat. For each* short-answer question, write your answer on the lines provided on the page. Stop when you reach the stop signs and wait for me to tell you to go on. When you have finished, put down your pencils and look at me. You may begin now.

Have children answer questions 4 through 24 and stop on page 15.

Phonics,
pages 16–17

Have children turn to page 16. Say: *I will say the name of each picture. After I say the name, read the four answer choices. Fill in the oval next to the word that names the picture. Mark your answers very carefully and make your marks dark and neat. Are there any questions?*

Respond to any questions.

Say: *Look at Number 25. I will say the name of the picture now. "Tree." "Tree." Read the four answer choices and fill in the bubble next to the word "Tree."*

Pause for students to mark their answers.

Say: *We will continue in the same way.*

Number 26: Drum

Number 27: Haystack

Number 28: Pie

Number 29: Rowboat

Number 30: Toast

Say: *Now put your pencils down and look at me.*

Writing,
pages 18–21

Have children turn to pages 18–19. Say: *Look at the writing prompt on page 18. It is followed by planning page 19. Use this blank page to plan your composition. You may want to make notes to decide what to write. You may want to make a web to put your ideas in an order that makes sense. You may want to write a rough draft. Remember that the more planning you do, the clearer your composition will be.*

Have children turn to pages 20–21. Say: *When you are ready to write your composition, be sure to write on answer document pages 20 and 21, which are the two pages with lines. Your composition does not have to completely fill these two lined pages, but it must not be longer than the two pages.*

Make sure children know what they are expected to do.

Say: *When you have finished writing, put down your pencil and look at me. You may begin writing now.*

Student Name _____

Date _____

Unit
Assessment
TESTED SKILLS AND STRATEGIES

- Listening Comprehension
- Reading Comprehension
- Vocabulary Strategies
- Literary Elements
- Text Features and Study Skills
- Grammar, Mechanics, and Usage
- Phonics
- Writing

Macmillan/McGraw-Hill

DIRECTIONS
Listen as your teacher reads the selection. Then read each question. Decide which is the best answer to each question. Mark the space for the answer you have chosen.

1 Sarah drew a red border on her poster to —

   A show that red is her favorite color

   B correct spelling mistakes

   C help children see the poster

   D make sure no one would see it

2 Which detail supports the idea that hamsters are good pets?

   A Hamsters are cute and friendly.

   B Sarah smoothed out her poster.

   C The hamsters will be gone soon.

   D Rags has eight babies.

3 Why did Sarah make her poster?

   A She found a good spot on the bulletin board.

   B She wanted to give away baby hamsters.

   C She liked to draw pictures of hamsters.

   D She knew that hamsters are easy to care for.

© Macmillan/McGraw-Hill

STOP

DIRECTIONS

Read each selection. Then read each question that follows
that selection. Decide which is the best answer to each question.
Mark the space for the answer you have chosen. Write your
answers to questions 8 and 14.

How to Make a Bird Feeder

1   How can you get birds to visit your yard? Put up a bird
feeder! A bird feeder is easy to make. You can make a bird
feeder with a pine cone or a milk jug.

2   To make a pine-cone feeder, you will need a pine cone, wire,
peanut butter, and birdseed.

3   First, find a large pine cone. Have an adult help you tie a
piece of wire to the pine cone. You will hang the bird feeder
from the wire.

4   Next, <u>smear</u> peanut butter all over the pine cone. Try to get
it into all the cracks. It might look yummy, but do not eat it!

5   Put birdseed into a dish. Roll the pine cone in it. Make sure
to cover the pine cone with birdseed. You now have a pine-
cone bird feeder!

6   To make a milk-jug feeder, you will need a milk jug, wire,
and birdseed.

7   First, have an adult help you cut a hole in the side of the
jug. Make sure it is large enough for a bird to fit inside.

8   Next, pour birdseed into the bottom of the jug. Make sure
the cap is still on the jug. The cap will help keep out rain.

9   Put the wire around the jug's handle. You now have a
milk-jug bird feeder!

GO ON ➡

Page 3

10   Have an adult help you hang your bird feeder high in a tree. Finally, sit quietly and <u>watch</u> the birds come to eat the birdseed.

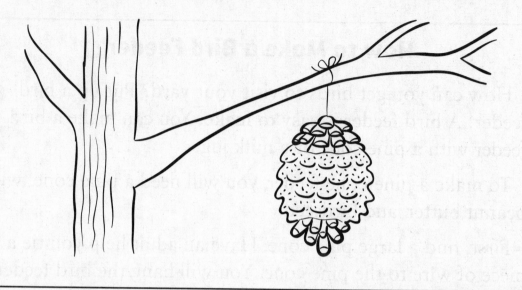

4 The main idea of the article is that —

    A birdseed sticks to peanut butter

    B you can hang a bird feeder with wire

    C the cap helps keep out rain

    D a bird feeder is easy to make

5 Which word means almost the same thing as <u>smear</u> in paragraph 4?

    A Spread

    B Eat

    C Remove

    D Wash

Page 4

GO ON ▶

6 What do you need to make a pine-cone bird feeder?

(A) Peanut Butter

(B) Cap

(C) Milk Jug

(D) Tree

7 In paragraph 10, the word <u>watch</u> means —

(A) look at

(B) wait for

(C) take care of

(D) a wrist clock

8 How are pine-cone feeders like milk-jug feeders? Use details from the article to support your answer.

_____

_____

_____

_____

GO ON

Page 5

The Zoo Train

1   "Hurry, Laura!" said Sono. "The <u>train</u> is about to leave!" The children were boarding the zoo train. Laura was sitting at the picnic table. Laura quickly packed up her lunch. She still had nuts to eat, but she did not want to miss the train. Laura put the nuts in her pocket. She ran to the train.

2   "All aboard!" called Billy. Laura got on board and sat in her seat. This was her first trip on the zoo train!

3   Slowly the train went through the park. Laura looked out and saw the park. Then the train went faster. The <u>wind</u> whipped Laura's pigtails. She felt <u>fearful</u> because the train was fast.

4   The train went slower when it turned a corner. Laura felt better. Now she could see the zoo! The children on the train could watch trees and animals. They saw a waterfall and petting zoo.

5   After a while, the train stopped. It was snack time now. Laura reached in her pocket. The nuts were gone! They must have fallen out when she ran. Then Laura saw a squirrel in the grass. It was eating a nut. "Look! The squirrel has my snack!" cried Laura.

6   The children went back to the picnic table to eat their snacks. Eva said, "You shared with the squirrel. So I will share with you!" Then Eva gave Laura half of her pear. Laura smiled and took a big bite.

Page 6

GO ON ➡

9 Look at the chart.

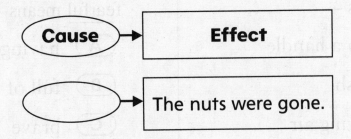

Which of these goes in the empty oval?

(A) The nuts fell out of Laura's pocket when she ran.

(B) Laura was sitting at the picnic table eating lunch.

(C) Laura saw a squirrel in the grass.

(D) It was snack time now.

---

10 Which word is in the same word family as the word <u>train</u> in paragraph 1?

(A) Brain

(B) Trail

(C) Tired

(D) Car

11 Why did Eva share her pear?

(A) Laura ran to the train.

(B) Laura felt scared.

(C) The squirrel ate Laura's nuts.

(D) The train stopped at snack time.

GO ON ▶

12 In paragraph 3, the word <u>wind</u> means —

(A) turn a handle

(B) brush

(C) moving air

(D) a cloud

13 In paragraph 3, the word <u>fearful</u> means —

(A) having no fear

(B) full of fear

(C) brave

(D) full of hope

14 How did Laura feel about her trip on the zoo train? Use details from the story to support your answer.

_____

_____

_____

_____

GO ON ▶

DIRECTIONS

Read the poem. Then read each question that follows the poem. Decide which is the best answer to each question. Mark the space for the answer you have chosen.

The Bird

1   Overhead, way up high,
2   I see a speckle in the sky.
3   It swoops down and I see,
4   A bird is heading to the tree.

5   To its small nest it flies,
6   It must have heard the babies' cries.
7   Worm dangles from its beak,
8   For the babies who chirp and squeak.

GO ON

Page 9

15 Which words from the poem rhyme?

    A *beak* and *sky*

    B *speckle* and *nest*

    C *tree* and *bird*

    D *cries* and *flies*

16 Which line from the poem has six beats?

    A Line 2

    B Line 3

    C Line 6

    D Line 8

STOP

Student Name _____

DIRECTIONS
Decide which is the best answer to each question. Mark the space for the answer you have chosen.

17 Look at the map.

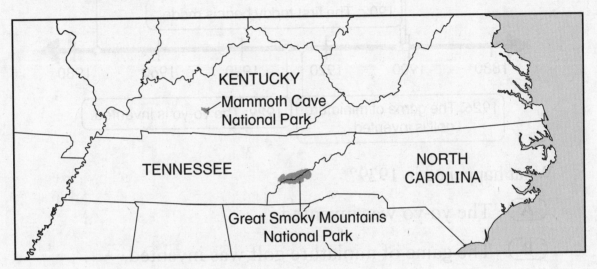

Where is Mammoth Cave National Park located?

- Ⓐ Kentucky
- Ⓑ Tennessee
- Ⓒ North Carolina
- Ⓓ Virginia

GO ON ➡

Page 11

18 Look at the time line.

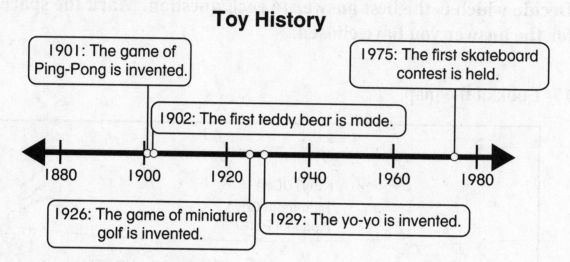

Toy History

1901: The game of Ping-Pong is invented.

1902: The first teddy bear is made.

1975: The first skateboard contest is held.

1880   1900   1920   1940   1960   1980

1926: The game of miniature golf is invented.

1929: The yo-yo is invented.

What happened in 1929?

(A) The yo-yo was invented.

(B) The game of miniature golf was invented.

(C) The first skateboard contest was held.

(D) The first teddy bear was made.

GO ON

19 Look at the picture and caption.

In basketball, players score points by putting the ball into the basket.

What is about to happen in the game?

(A) The white team is about to score.

(B) The black team is about to score.

(C) The game is about to start.

(D) Snacks are about to be served.

20 Look at the table of contents.

You would find information about gerbils on page —

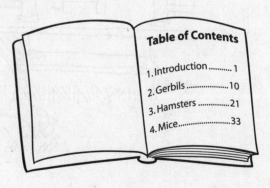

Table of Contents

(A) 1

(B) 10

(C) 23

(D) 34

STOP

DIRECTIONS

Read the introduction and the passage that follows. Then read each question and fill in the correct answer.

Alex wrote this story about a visit to a farm. He wants you to review his story. As you read, think about the corrections and improvements Alex should make. Then answer the questions that follow.

Chickens Everywhere

(1) Laura visited her aunts farm. (2) The farm was in arkansas. (3) Birds animals and crops lived on it. (4) She saw many chickens on the farm. (5) Some chickens sat on fences and in treees. (6) Laura even saw a chicken sitting on a chair!

Page 14

GO ON ➡

21 What is the **BEST** way to write sentence 1?

(A) Laura visited her aunts farm.

(B) Laura visited her aunt's farm.

(C) Laura visited her 'aunts' farm.

(D) Laura visited her aunt,s farm.

22 What is the **BEST** way to write sentence 2?

(A) The farm was in arkansas.

(B) The farm was in arKansas.

(C) The Farm was in arkansas.

(D) The farm was in Arkansas.

23 What is the **BEST** way to write sentence 3?

(A) Birds, animals, and crops lived on it.

(B) Birds animals, and crops lived on it.

(C) Birds animals and crops lived on it.

(D) Birds, animals and crops, lived on it.

24 What is the **BEST** way to write sentence 5?

(A) Some chickens sat on fences and in trees.

(B) Some chickens sat on fences and in tree's.

(C) Some chickens sat on fences and in trees.'

(D) Some chickens sat on fences and in treees.

Page 15

STOP

DIRECTIONS
Mark the space for the word that names the picture.

25

(A) Three

(B) Tray

(C) Trumpet

(D) Tree

26

(A) Dim

(B) Gum

(C) Drum

(D) Dresses

27

(A) Hat

(B) Haystack

(C) Hoe

(D) High

28

- (A) Sky
- (B) Pie
- (C) Pay
- (D) Pine cone

29

- (A) Rowboat
- (B) Runway
- (C) Toe
- (D) Road

30

- (A) Total
- (B) Toes
- (C) Toss
- (D) Toast

STOP

WRITTEN COMPOSITION

> Write a how-to article that tells
> how to play a playground game.

The information in the box below will help you remember what you should think about when you write your composition.

REMEMBER TO –

- write about how to play a playground game

- make sure that every sentence you write helps the reader understand your composition

- include enough details to help the reader clearly understand what you are saying

- use correct spelling, capitalization, punctuation, grammar, and sentences

Page 18

Student Name _____

Student Name

USE THIS PREWRITING PAGE TO
PLAN YOUR COMPOSITION

MAKE SURE THAT YOU WRITE YOUR COMPOSITION ON
THE LINES ON PAGES 20-21

Page 19

Answer Document

_____

_____

_____

_____

_____

_____

_____

_____

_____

Answer Document

_____

_____

_____

_____

_____

_____

_____

_____

_____

Page 21

Student Name_____

Student Evaluation Chart

Tested Skills	Number Correct	Percent Correct
Listening Comprehension: *Character*, 1; *Main Idea and Details*, 2; *Cause and Effect*, 3	/3	%
Reading Comprehension: *Main Idea and Details*, 4, 6; *Character*, 9; *Cause and Effect*, 11	/4	%
Short answer: *Compare and Contrast*, 8; *Make Inferences*, 14	/6	%
Vocabulary Strategies: *Context Clues*, 5; *Context Clues: Multiple-Meaning Words*, 7, 12; *Word Parts: Word Families*, 10; *Word Parts: Suffixes*, 13	/5	%
Literary Elements: *Rhyme*, 15; *Rhythmic Patterns*, 16	/2	%
Text Features and Study Skills: *Maps*, 17; *Time Lines*, 18; *Photos and Captions*, 19; *Using Parts of a Book*, 20	/4	%
Grammar, Mechanics, and Usage: *Possessive Nouns*, 21; *Proper Nouns*, 22; *Using Commas in a Series*, 23; *Plural Nouns*, 24	/4	%
Phonics: *Consonant Blend* tr-, 25; *Consonant Blend* dr-, 26; *Long a, ay*, 27; *Long i, ie*, 28; *Long o, ow*, 29; *Long o, oa*, 30	/6	%
Writing: *How-to Article*	/4	%
Total Unit Test Score	/38	%

This Unit Assessment is designed to measure your children's mastery of the skills taught in the unit. The test assesses all of the following areas:

- Listening Comprehension
- Reading Comprehension
- Vocabulary Strategies
- Literary Elements
- Text Features and Study Skills
- Grammar, Mechanics, and Usage
- Phonics
- Writing

Listening Comprehension, page 2

Say: *Listen while I read this story to you. You will be asked to answer three multiple-choice questions based on this story. Listen carefully. We will begin now.*

An Unusual Map

An artist named Ruth Asawa had an idea for making an unusual map of San Francisco. She wanted people to work together to create something beautiful.

First, Ruth drew a map on paper. Then she mixed together flour, salt, and water to make clay. Next Ruth and her friends began making little people and buildings out of the clay. They put them on the map.

School kids helped them make more buildings and people. Some children used the clay to make a model of their school. Then other children and Ruth's friends helped make models of their homes, cars, and even themselves. Over two hundred people helped make Ruth's map! The clay map became very large.

Two years later Ruth Asawa made a copy of the map out of metal. She used the metal map to make a large, round fountain. Now the map is outdoors for people in San Francisco to see and enjoy.

Now have children turn to page 2 and read the directions at the top of the page. Then say: *Answer questions 1–3 on page 2. Read each question carefully. To answer a question, fill in the oval next to the answer you have chosen. Mark only one oval for each question. Make your marks dark and neat. Stop when you reach the stop sign on the bottom of page 2. When you have finished, put down your pencils and look at me. You may begin now.*

Have children answer questions 1 through 3 and stop on page 2.

Reading Comprehension; Vocabulary Strategies; Literary Elements; Text Features and Study Skills; Grammar, Mechanics, and Usage, pages 3–15

Have children turn to page 3. Say: *You will now answer some multiple-choice and short-answer questions. Read all of the selections and questions carefully. You will see that the paragraphs in the reading selections and the lines in the poem are numbered. There also is a number before each sentence in the passage on page 14. These numbers will help you find the sentence or sentences you will need to answer the questions that follow. For each multiple-choice question, read all four answer choices. To answer a multiple-choice question, fill in the oval next to the answer you have* chosen. Mark only one oval for each question. Make your marks dark and neat. For each short-answer question, write your answer on the lines provided on the page. Stop when you reach the stop signs and wait for me to tell you to go on. When you have finished, put down your pencils and look at me. You may begin now.

Have children answer questions 4 through 24 and stop on page 15.

Phonics,
pages 16–17

Have children turn to page 16. Say: *I will say the name of each picture. After I say the name, read the four answer choices. Fill in the oval next to the word that names the picture. Mark your answers very carefully and make your marks dark and neat. Are there any questions?*

Respond to any questions.

Say: *Look at Number 25. I will say the name of the picture now. "Lambs." "Lambs." Read the four answer choices and fill in the oval next to the word "Lambs."*

Pause for children to mark their answers.

Say: *We will continue in the same way.*

Number 26: Chair

Number 27: Bird

Number 28: Wristwatch

Number 29: Core

Number 30: Deer

Say: *Now put your pencils down and look at me.*

Writing,
pages 18–21

Have children turn to pages 18–19. Say: *Look at the writing prompt on page 18. It is followed by planning page 19. Use this blank page to plan your composition. You may want to make notes to decide what to write. You may want to make a web to put your ideas in an order that makes sense. You may want to write a rough draft. Remember that the more planning you do, the clearer your composition will be.*

Have children turn to pages 20–21. Say: *When you are ready to write your composition, be sure to write on answer document pages 20 and 21, which are the two pages with lines. Your composition does not have to completely fill these two lined pages, but it must not be longer than the two pages.*

Make sure children know what they are expected to do.

Say: *When you have finished writing, put down your pencil and look at me. You may begin writing now.*

Student Name _____

Date _____

Unit Assessment

TESTED SKILLS AND STRATEGIES

- **Listening Comprehension**
- **Reading Comprehension**
- **Vocabulary Strategies**
- **Literary Elements**
- **Text Features and Study Skills**
- **Grammar, Mechanics, and Usage**
- **Phonics**
- **Writing**

Macmillan/McGraw-Hill

DIRECTIONS

Listen as your teacher reads the selection. Then read each question. Decide which is the best answer to each question. Mark the space for the answer you have chosen.

1 What is the best summary of this article?

(A) Ruth Asawa wanted to make a map. Many people worked together to make it. Then she made it into a fountain.

(B) School kids helped make models of buildings. They worked together to make them. Ruth Asawa helped.

(C) Ruth Asawa is an artist. She lives in San Francisco. She makes paintings.

(D) Ruth Asawa made a fountain. Then she mixed up clay. She made a model of the ocean with it.

2 Which ingredients did Ruth use to make her clay?

(A) Flour, sugar, water

(B) Flour, salt, oil

(C) Flour, salt, water

(D) Dirt, salt, water

3 The author wrote this article to help readers —

(A) learn about maps

(B) know how to make clay

(C) plan a visit to San Francisco to see Ruth Asawa's special map

(D) learn about people working together to make something special

STOP

DIRECTIONS

Read each selection. Then read each question that follows that selection. Decide which is the best answer to each question. Mark the space for the answer you have chosen. Write your answers to questions 8 and 14.

Jam Day

1   It is early in the morning. Tim has been up for a long time. For Tim, this is just about the best day of the year. He and his family are going to the country to pick blackberries. His mother and father call it Jam Day. Everybody will help pick the blackberries. Then Mother will make enough jam to <u>last</u> all year.

2   Tim's friend Ray will come along this year. It will be Ray's first Jam Day. The day is sunny and warm, and the bushes are full of blackberries.

3   Tim and Ray start to work right away, and Tim is surprised how fast Ray can pick blackberries. Tim remembers that it took him quite a while to learn.

GO ON

4   Later, there are <u>pails</u> of blackberries everywhere. Tim goes over to his father. "Look at all the blackberries Ray picked, Dad. This is his first Jam Day. And he has just as many buckets as you have."

5   Dad is silent for a minute. "You are right, Tim. Ray has done a great job. How did you learn to pick blackberries so fast, Ray?"

6   Ray replied "I worked very hard. I tried to make up for all the jam I've had at your house."

---

4 In paragraph 4, why were pails of blackberries everywhere?

   Ⓐ Other blackberry pickers had left them there.

   Ⓑ Everyone had picked lots of blackberries.

   Ⓒ They had forgotten to put away the pails.

   Ⓓ They had woken up early in the morning.

5 In paragraph 1, the word <u>last</u> means —

   Ⓐ grow

   Ⓑ finish

   Ⓒ waste

   Ⓓ have

© Macmillan/McGraw-Hill

GO ON ➡

6 Why is Tim surprised in paragraph 3?

    A Mother makes jam.

    B The jam lasts all year.

    C Dad is silent for a minute.

    D Ray picks blackberries quickly.

7 Which word from a thesaurus has the same meaning as <u>pails</u> in paragraph 4?

    A Buckets

    B Hoses

    C Early

    D Pale

8 What happens on Jam Day? Explain your answer and support it with details from the story.

_____

_____

_____

_____

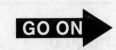

The Story of Popcorn

1　　A <u>handful</u> of popcorn is a good snack. People have eaten popcorn for a long time. Popcorn has even been found in old, old caves.

2　　American Indians probably had the first popcorn. They invented the first popcorn maker. They heated rocks in a big fire. Then, they put the seeds of corn on the rocks until the corn popped. Sometimes the popped corn would fly off the rocks! They had to try to catch it quickly.

3　　Some people put oil on an ear of corn. They held it on a stick over a fire. The corn popped on the ear. Then, they <u>chewed</u> the popcorn right off the ear.

4　　When Europeans came to America, they learned about popcorn. They liked to eat it for breakfast. They filled a bowl with popcorn and <u>poured</u> milk on it. It was breakfast cereal.

5　　Corn will not pop until it is very hot. Popcorn seeds are wet inside. When the seed gets hot, they pop. A piece of popcorn can get up to 40 times bigger when it pops. If a popcorn seed does not have enough water, it will not pop. Those are the seeds you see in the bottom of a bag of popcorn.

Page 6

GO ON ▶

9 Look at the chart.

Fact Popcorn seeds without enough water won't pop.	Fact The seeds at the bottom of the bag did not pop.

Conclusion

Which of these goes in the *Conclusion* box?

A The seeds at the bottom had enough water.

B The seeds at the bottom popped.

C The seeds are at the top of the bag.

D The seeds at the bottom did not have enough water.

10 In paragraph 1, the word <u>handful</u> means —

A a fist

B a hand letting go

C as much as a hand can hold

D as much as five hands can hold

11 The author wrote "The Story of Popcorn" to —

A inform readers about the history of popcorn

B scare readers with a spooky story

C persuade readers to eat popcorn for breakfast

D entertain readers with jokes

GO ON

Page 7

12 Which word from a thesaurus has the same meaning as <u>chewed</u> in paragraph 3?

- (A) Nibbled
- (B) Cooked
- (C) Chanted
- (D) Grew

13 Which words in paragraph 4 help you understand what <u>poured</u> means?

- (A) *They, with*
- (B) *liked, eat*
- (C) *popcorn, it*
- (D) *bowl, milk*

14 Write a summary of "The Story of Popcorn." Support your answer with details from the article.

_____

_____

_____

_____

Page 8

GO ON ▶

Unit Assessment

DIRECTIONS

Read the poem. Then read each question that follows the poem. Decide which is the best answer to each question. Mark the space for the answer you have chosen.

Spaghetti

1   The pot on the stovetop
2   Gurgles and bubbles.
3   My mom says it's time to
4   toss in the noodles.

5   Splish! Splash!
6   I drop them in the water.
7   Tick! Tick!
8   I wind and watch the timer.
9   Ding-a-ling! Ding-a-ling ding!

10   The timer says they're done.
11   Now I enjoy my noodles
12   Around my fork they're spun.

GO ON ➤

15 Which line from the poem uses alliteration?

- **A** Line 2
- **B** Line 4
- **C** Line 8
- **D** Line 12

16 Which word from the poem is an example of onomatopoeia?

- **A** *Splish*
- **B** *fork*
- **C** *Around*
- **D** *stovetop*

STOP

DIRECTIONS

Decide which is the best answer to each question. Mark the space for the answer you have chosen.

Use the graph to answer questions 17 and 18.

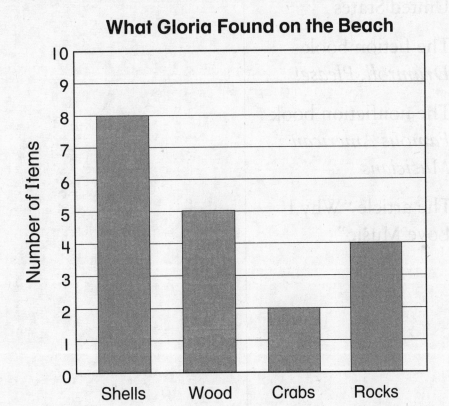

What Gloria Found on the Beach

17 How many more shells than rocks did Gloria find on the beach?

- **A** 1
- **B** 0
- **C** 2
- **D** 4

18 Gloria found 2 fewer crabs than —

- **A** rocks
- **B** shells
- **C** wood
- **D** crabs

Page 11

19 Which resource should you pick if you need to research American musicians?

(A) An atlas of the United States

(B) The fiction book *Drumroll, Please!*

(C) The nonfiction book *Famous American Musicians*

(D) The article "Why I Love Music"

20 Look at the Web page.

Pet Animals ▼

Mouse

> **Size**

A mouse is 2-3 inches long. It also has a long tail.

> **Food**

Mice can eat pellets from the pet store, grains, or seeds. Don't feed your mouse food such as candy and chips.

> **Care**

Mice do not like to be alone. You should keep two in a cage so that they can keep each other company.

In which section would you find information about what to feed a pet mouse?

(A) Pet Animals

(B) Care

(C) Size

(D) Food

STOP

Page 13

DIRECTIONS
Read the introduction and the passage that follows. Then read each question and fill in the correct answer.

Noah wrote this story about a visit to the doctor. He wants you to review his story. As you read, think about the corrections and improvements Noah should make. Then answer the questions that follow.

My Check-Up

(1) I am waiting to see Dr Wing. (2) His waiting room many books and toys. (3) Last time, I look at a book about bones. (4) This time, I read a book titled <u>good germs, Bad Germs</u>. (5) I learn how to stay healthy.

© Macmillan/McGraw-Hill

21 What is the **BEST** way to revise sentence 1?

    A I am waiting to see Dr' Wing.

    B I am waiting to see Dr, Wing.

    C I am waiting to see Dr. Wing.

    D I am waiting to see Dr! Wing.

22 What is the **BEST** way to revise sentence 2?

    A His waiting room have many books and toys.

    B His waiting room haves many books and toys.

    C His waiting room is have many books and toys.

    D His waiting room has many books and toys.

23 What is the **BEST** way to revise sentence 3?

    A Last time, I was look at a book about bones.

    B Last time, I looks at a book about bones.

    C Last time, I is looking at a book about bones.

    D Last time, I looked at a book about bones.

24 What change, if any, should be made to sentence 4?

    A Change the comma to a period

    B Change *read* to **red**

    C Change *good germs* to **Good Germs**

    D Make no change

STOP

DIRECTIONS
Mark the space for the word that names the picture.

25
(A) Ladies
(B) Lands
(C) Lamps
(D) Lambs

26
(A) Bear
(B) Chart
(C) Cherry
(D) Chair

27
(A) Bite
(B) Butter
(C) Bird
(D) Born

28

- Ⓐ Wreck
- Ⓑ Writing
- Ⓒ Wrap
- Ⓓ Wristwatch

29

- Ⓐ Cove
- Ⓑ Born
- Ⓒ Cone
- Ⓓ Core

30

- Ⓐ Dare
- Ⓑ Tear
- Ⓒ Cheery
- Ⓓ Deer

STOP

Page 17

WRITTEN COMPOSITION

Write a letter to persuade your teacher to take the class on a field trip to your favorite place.

The information in the box below will help you remember what you should think about when you write your composition.

REMEMBER TO –

- write about why the class should take a trip to your favorite place

- make sure that every sentence you write helps the reader understand your composition

- include enough details to help the reader clearly understand what you are saying

- use correct spelling, capitalization, punctuation, grammar, and sentences

Page 18

Student Name _____

Student Name

```
┌─────────────────────────────────────────┐
│         USE THIS PREWRITING PAGE TO       │
│         PLAN YOUR COMPOSITION             │
└─────────────────────────────────────────┘
```

```
┌─────────────────────────────────────────┐
│  MAKE SURE THAT YOU WRITE YOUR COMPOSITION ON │
│         THE LINES ON PAGES 20-21          │
└─────────────────────────────────────────┘
```

Page 19

Answer Document

_____

_____

_____

_____

_____

_____

_____

_____

_____

© Macmillan/McGraw-Hill

Page 20

Student Name _____

Answer Document

_____

_____

_____

_____

_____

_____

_____

_____

_____

Page 21

Student Name_____

Grade 2 • Unit 3
Student Evaluation Chart

Tested Skills	Number Correct	Percent Correct
Listening Comprehension: *Summarize, 1; Main Idea and Details, 2; Author's Purpose, 3*	/3	%
Reading Comprehension: *Cause and Effect, 4, 6; Draw Conclusions, 9; Author's Purpose, 11*	/4	%
Short answer: *Summarize, 8, 14*	/6	%
Vocabulary Strategies: *Context Clues: Multiple-Meaning Words, 5; Thesaurus, 7, 12; Word Parts: Suffixes, 10; Context Clues, 13*	/5	%
Literary Elements: *Alliteration, 15; Onomatopoeia, 16*	/2	%
Text Features and Study Skills: *Bar Graphs, 17, 18; Choose Research Materials, 19; Headings, 20*	/4	%
Grammar, Mechanics, and Usage: *Abbreviations, 21; The Verb have, 22; Past-Tense Verbs, 23; Book Titles, 24*	/4	%
Phonics: *Silent Letters -mb, 25; r-Controlled Vowels, 26, 27, 28, 29, 30*	/6	%
Writing: *Persuasive Letter*	/4	%
Total Unit Test Score	/38	%

This Unit Assessment is designed to measure your children's mastery of the skills taught in the unit. The test assesses all of the following areas:

- Listening Comprehension
- Reading Comprehension
- Vocabulary Strategies
- Literary Elements
- Text Features and Study Skills
- Grammar, Mechanics, and Usage
- Phonics
- Writing

Listening Comprehension, page 2

Say: *Listen while I read this story to you. You will be asked to answer three multiple-choice questions based on this story. Listen carefully. We will begin now.*

The True Story of Seabiscuit

Seabiscuit was one of the most famous racehorses of all time. Seabiscuit did not look like other racehorses. Most racehorses have long legs and a long tail. Seabiscuit had short legs and a short tail. One of his front legs turned when he ran.

When Seabiscuit was young, he ran in many races. The riders would often whip him. Seabiscuit was nervous. One rider said Seabiscuit was mean. After three years of not running very fast, Seabiscuit was sold.

The new owner was different. He fed Seabiscuit special hay. He put Seabiscuit in a stall with a calm horse. He did not whip his horses.

Seabiscuit began winning races. He became one of the top horses in the country. Then he was set to race against the champion, War Admiral. No one thought Seabiscuit could win. At the start, Seabiscuit ran ahead of War Admiral. On the last turn, Seabiscuit slowed down and War Admiral caught up. Then Seabiscuit looked over at War Admiral and ran faster. Seabiscuit won!

Now have children turn to page 2 and read the directions at the top of the page. Then say: *Answer questions 1–3 on page 2. Read each question carefully. To answer a question, fill in the oval next to the answer you have chosen. Mark only one oval for each question. Make your marks dark and neat. Stop when you reach the stop sign on the bottom of page 2. When you have finished, put down your pencils and look at me. You may begin now.*

Have children answer questions 1 through 3 and stop on page 2.

Reading Comprehension; Vocabulary Strategies; Literary Elements; Text Features and Study Skills; Grammar, Mechanics, and Usage, pages 3–15

Have children turn to page 3. Say: *You will now answer some multiple-choice and short-answer questions. Read all of the selections and questions carefully. You will see that the paragraphs in the reading selections and the lines in the poem are numbered. There also is a number before each sentence in the passage on page 14. These numbers will help you find the sentence or sentences you will need to answer the questions that follow. For each*

© Macmillan/McGraw-Hill

multiple-choice question, read all four answer choices. To answer a multiple-choice question, fill in the oval next to the answer you have chosen. Mark only one oval for each question. Make your marks dark and neat. For each short-answer question, write your answer on the lines provided on the page. Stop when you reach the stop signs and wait for me to tell you to go on. When you have finished, put down your pencils and look at me. You may begin now._

Have children answer questions 4 through 24 and stop on page 15.

Phonics,
pages 16–17

Have children turn to page 16. Say: _I will say the name of each picture. After I say the name, read the four answer choices. Fill in the oval next to the word that names the picture. Mark your answers very carefully and make your marks dark and neat. Are there any questions?_

Respond to any questions.

Say: _Look at Number 25. I will say the name of the picture now. "Cow." "Cow." Read the four answer choices and fill in the oval next to the word "Cow."_

Pause for children to mark their answers.

Say: _We will continue in the same way._

Number 26: Toy

Number 27: Moon

Number 28: Paws

Number 29: Book

Number 30: Teaspoon

Say: _Now put your pencils down and look at me._

Writing,
pages 18–21

Have children turn to pages 18–19. Say: _Look at the writing prompt on page 18. It is followed by planning page 19. Use this blank page to plan your composition. You may want to make notes to decide what to write. You may want to make a web to put your ideas in an order that makes sense. You may want to write a rough draft. Remember that the more planning you do, the clearer your composition will be._

Have children turn to pages 20–21. Say: _When you are ready to write your composition, be sure to write on answer document pages 20 and 21, which are the two pages with lines. Your composition does not have to completely fill these two lined pages, but it must not be longer than the two pages._

Make sure children know what they are expected to do.

Say: _When you have finished writing, put down your pencil and look at me. You may begin writing now._

Student Name _____

Date _____

Unit Assessment
TESTED SKILLS AND STRATEGIES

- **Listening Comprehension**
- **Reading Comprehension**
- **Vocabulary Strategies**
- **Literary Elements**
- **Text Features and Study Skills**
- **Grammar, Mechanics, and Usage**
- **Phonics**
- **Writing**

Mc Graw Hill **Macmillan/McGraw-Hill**

DIRECTIONS

Listen as your teacher reads the selection. Then read each question. Decide which is the best answer to each question. Mark the space for the answer you have chosen.

1 Seabiscuit was sold after —

    (A) three years of not running very fast

    (B) he was set to race the champion

    (C) War Admiral caught up

    (D) he began winning races

2 The author wrote this article to —

    (A) persuade people not to sell horses

    (B) inform people about War Admiral

    (C) help Seabiscuit win the race

    (D) tell people about a special racehorse

3 How do you know that this article is nonfiction?

    (A) It has made-up characters.

    (B) The events really happened.

    (C) It is about a horse.

    (D) It has a plot and setting.

Page 2

STOP

DIRECTIONS

Read each selection. Then read each question that follows that selection. Decide which is the best answer to each question. Mark the space for the answer you have chosen. Write your answers to questions 8 and 14.

Help from the Paramedics

1   Paramedics are people who are trained to help others. Often people become ill or have accidents when there is no doctor around to care for them. Time may be important. They call 911 for help. The 911 workers get help for the hurt or sick person. The people who come to help often are the paramedics.

2   Many paramedics are also <u>firefighters</u>. Other people can learn to become paramedics, too. Training is long and hard. They spend months in classes taught by doctors. Paramedics also practice their skills. This helps them learn what their job is all about. The training and practice make them ready to help people.

3   Paramedics come by ambulance or fire truck. They work in teams of two. One person calls the hospital to get help from a doctor. The other person works with the sick person as the doctor tells them what to do. Often the sick person must go to a hospital. The person travels to the hospital in the ambulance. The paramedics ride along to help the person. They make sure that all goes well until a doctor takes over at the hospital.

GO ON

Page 3

4 Paramedics must make sure that the ambulance is always clean and has <u>supplies</u>. They check the ambulance after they take care of each sick person. Then they head off to help the next person who needs their help.

4 Before people become paramedics, they —

   A call 911 for help

   B work in teams of two

   C spend months in classes taught by doctors

   D travel to the hospital in an ambulance

5 In paragraph 2, the word <u>firefighters</u> means —

   A people who fight fires

   B people who use fire to fight

   C people who are very angry

   D people who are hurt or sick

GO ON ➡

Page 4

6 What is this article mainly about?

    A You can call 911 for help in an emergency.

    B Paramedics can also be firefighters.

    C Training for paramedics is long and hard.

    D Paramedics do many things to help people.

7 What is the base word for <u>supplies</u> in paragraph 4?

    A supply

    B supplie

    C supplys

    D supplying

8 What happens after someone calls 911? Explain your answer and support it with details from the article.

_____

_____

_____

_____

© Macmillan/McGraw-Hill

Page 5

The Elves and the Shoemaker

1   There was once a kind <u>shoemaker</u> who was very poor. He had no money to buy food or wood for the fire.

2   The day came when he had only enough leather to make one <u>pair</u> of shoes. He cut the leather and went to bed. The next morning instead of the leather, he found a beautiful pair of shoes! Just then a rich man came in. He saw the shoes and paid a lot of money.

3   With the money, the shoemaker bought leather to make four more pairs of shoes. The next morning, he saw four perfect pairs of shoes. Then four men came and bought the shoes.

4   With the money the shoemaker bought more leather. Just as before, new shoes appeared the next morning and <u>customers</u> bought them. It went on like this for quite some time.

5   "I wonder who is making these shoes," the shoemaker's wife said one day. So the two waited up to see. At midnight they saw two elves dressed in rags. They watched the elves make many pairs of fine shoes.

6   "Poor elves," said the shoemaker's wife. "They have made us rich and yet they have nothing to wear but rags." So she made them each a tiny suit and left the clothes in the workroom.

© Macmillan/McGraw-Hill

Page 6

GO ON ▶

7   At midnight, the elves came in. They put on the clothes and danced and laughed. Soon they danced out the door. That was the last the shoemaker and his wife saw of them.

9 Look at the chart.

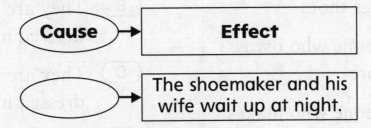

Which of these goes in the blank oval?

(A) They were too excited to sleep.

(B) They wondered who was making the shoes.

(C) They had no money left.

(D) Four men came to buy shoes.

10 In a dictionary, which word would be listed as a homophone of pair in paragraph 2?

(A) pear

(B) peer

(C) couple

(D) paired

11 In paragraph 4, the word customers means —

(A) people who buy things

(B) people who make shoes

(C) stores

(D) elves

Page 7

GO ON

12 In paragraph 1, the word <u>shoemaker</u> means —

  A someone who has lots of shoes

  B a machine that makes shoes

  C someone who owns a store

  D someone who makes shoes

13 Which statement best describes the elves in the illustration?

  A They are tiny and dressed in suits.

  B They are giants and dressed in suits.

  C They are tiny and dressed in rags.

  D They are giants and dressed in rags.

14 Is "The Elves and the Shoemaker" a fantasy or a true story? Explain your answer and support it with details from the story.

_____

_____

_____

_____

© Macmillan/McGraw-Hill

DIRECTIONS

Read the poem. Then read each question that follows the poem. Decide which is the best answer to each question. Mark the space for the answer you have chosen.

The Circus

1   The circus came when I was three.
2   Lights sparkled like diamonds at me.
3   The circus came when I was four.
4   A golden lion gave a roar!
5   The circus came when I was five.
6   People on ropes would swing and dive.
7   The circus came when I was six.
8   Painted clowns played funny tricks.
9   I am seven and I just know
10   Soon there will be a circus show!

15 Which line from the poem uses a simile?

- (A) Line 2
- (B) Line 4
- (C) Line 8
- (D) Line 10

16 Which words from the poem rhyme?

- (A) *six* and *tricks*
- (B) *circus* and *came*
- (C) *Soon* and *show*
- (D) *swing* and *seven*

STOP

DIRECTIONS
Decide which is the best answer to each question. Mark the space for the answer you have chosen.

17 Look at the drop-down menu.

Farm Animals

Dairy Farming

Farming: Then and Now

How to Sheep Farm

From Farm to Market

Which Web link would you select if you wanted to read about farming long ago?

(A) Dairy Farming

(B) How to Sheep Farm

(C) From Farm to Market

(D) Farming: Then and Now

GO ON

18 Look at the floor plan.

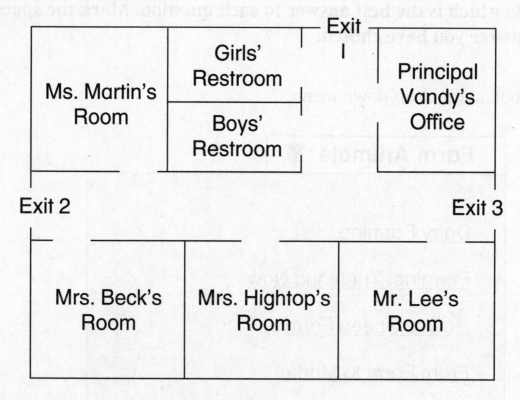

Which rooms are closest to Exit 3?

- (A) Mrs. Beck's and Mrs. Hightop's
- (B) Principal Vandy's and Mr. Lee's
- (C) Mr. Lee's and Mrs. Beck's
- (D) Mr. Lee's and Ms. Martin's

19 Look at the home page.

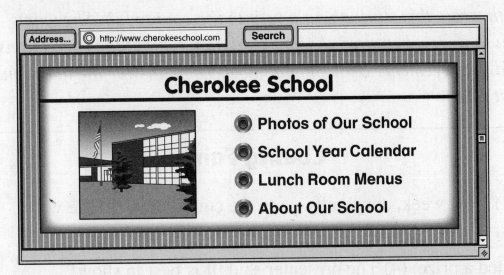

Which link would you click to find out what is for lunch?

(A) Photos of Our School

(B) School Year Calendar

(C) Lunch Room Menus

(D) About Our School

20 Look at the recipe. What should you do while the butter is melting?

(A) Break four eggs

(B) Turn over bread

(C) Beat the milk and eggs

(D) Put the bread in the egg mixture

French Toast

1. Break eggs into a pie pan.
2. Add milk and beat lightly.
3. Melt butter in a skillet.
4. While butter is melting, put bread into egg mixture.
5. Cook over medium heat in the skillet.

Page 13

© Macmillan/McGraw-Hill

Read the introduction and the passage that follows. Then read each question and fill in the correct answer.

Beth wrote this story about a visit to the county fair. She wants you to review her story. As you read, think about the corrections and improvements Beth should make. Then answer the questions that follow.

County Fair

(1) Next week, our family go to the county fair. (2) We will bring two sheep to enter in the show. (3) Last year, our sheep winned a prize. (4) The presenter said, It is best in show!"
(5) My friend Claire is going with us this year. (6) I cant wait!

GO ON

© Macmillan/McGraw-Hill

21 What is the **BEST** way to revise sentence 1?

(A) Next week, our family wills go to the county fair.

(B) Next week, our family is go to the county fair.

(C) Next week, our family will go to the county fair.

(D) Next week, our family go to the county fair.

22 What is the **BEST** way to revise sentence 3?

(A) Last year, our sheep wonned a prize.

(B) Last year, our sheep winning a prize.

(C) Last year, our sheep won a prize.

(D) Last year, our sheep will won a prize.

23 What change, if any, should be made to sentence 4?

(A) Insert a comma before *said*

(B) Change *presenter* to **Presenter**

(C) Add a quotation mark before *It*

(D) Make no change

24 What change, if any, should be made to sentence 6?

(A) Change *cant* to **can't**

(B) Change *I* to **i**

(C) Change *wait* to **wate**

(D) Make no change

STOP

DIRECTIONS
Mark the space for the word that names the picture.

25

(A) Car

(B) Cow

(C) Coy

(D) Cowboy

26

(A) Toast

(B) Tea

(C) Toy

(D) Toe

27

(A) Main

(B) Morning

(C) Mean

(D) Moon

28

- (A) Pie
- (B) Party
- (C) Pays
- (D) Paws

29

- (A) Book
- (B) Bake
- (C) Beak
- (D) Barking

30

- (A) Spun
- (B) Teaspoon
- (C) Spine
- (D) Teapot

STOP

WRITTEN COMPOSITION

Write a book report about a book you like.

The information in the box below will help you remember what you should think about when you write your composition.

REMEMBER TO –

- write about a book that you like

- make sure that every sentence you write helps the reader understand your composition

- include enough details to help the reader clearly understand what you are saying

- use correct spelling, capitalization, punctuation, grammar, and sentences

Page 18

USE THIS PREWRITING PAGE TO
PLAN YOUR COMPOSITION

MAKE SURE THAT YOU WRITE YOUR COMPOSITION ON
THE LINES ON PAGES 20-21

Answer Document

_____

_____

_____

_____

_____

_____

_____

_____

_____

Answer Document

_____

_____

_____

_____

_____

_____

_____

_____

_____

_____

Page 21

Student Name_____

Grade 2 • Unit 4
Student Evaluation Chart

Tested Skills	Number Correct	Percent Correct
Listening Comprehension: *Sequence of Events, 1; Author's Purpose, 2; Text Structure: Fiction Versus Nonfiction, 3*	/3	%
Reading Comprehension: *Sequence of Events, 4; Main Idea and Details, 6; Cause and Effect, 9; Use Illustrations, 13*	/4	%
Short answer: *Sequence of Events, 8; Distinguish Between Fantasy and Reality, 14*	/6	%
Vocabulary Strategies: *Word Parts: Compound Words, 5, 12; Word Parts: Base Words, 7; Dictionary: Homophones, 10; Context Clues, 11*	/5	%
Literary Elements: *Simile, 15; Rhyme, 16*	/2	%
Text Features and Study Skills: *Drop-Down Menus, 17; Floor Plan, 18; Using the Internet, 19; Written Directions, 20*	/4	%
Grammar, Mechanics, and Usage: *Helping Verbs, 21; Irregular Verbs, 22; Quotation Marks, 23; Contractions, 24*	/4	%
Phonics: *Vowel Diphthong -ow, 25; Vowel Diphthong -oy, 26; Vowel Digraph -oo, 27, 29, 30; Vowel Digraph -aw, 28*	/6	%
Writing: *Book Report*	/4	%
Total Unit Test Score	/38	%

© Macmillan/McGraw-Hill

Unit Assessment

This Unit Assessment is designed to measure your children's mastery of the skills taught in the unit. The test assesses all of the following areas:

- Listening Comprehension
- Reading Comprehension
- Vocabulary Strategies
- Literary Elements
- Text Features and Study Skills
- Grammar, Mechanics, and Usage
- Phonics
- Writing

Listening Comprehension, page 2

Say: *Listen while I read this story to you. You will be asked to answer three multiple-choice questions based on this story. Listen carefully. We will begin now.*

Sharing a Birthday

"I wish I weren't a twin," James shouted at his twin sister, Jennie."You don't even get a birthday to yourself!" He ran out of the house.

Her brother always complained about how hard it was to have a twin sister. Jennie continued to read her book. She knew he would get over it soon.

James sat in the yard. Then he saw Mr. Parrish next door carrying a brown box.

"What's in the box?" he asked.

"New kittens," said Mr. Parrish. "I am bringing them to the pet store."

James opened the lid. As soon as he saw the kittens he knew that was what he wanted for his birthday.

However, he knew that Mom and Dad would not let him have two kittens. "How sad it would be not to let them stay together," he thought.

Just then he had an idea. "Maybe Jennie would like a kitten, too," he thought. "If she would, I bet Mom and Dad would get us kittens for our birthday."

He ran inside to get Jennie and Mom."That's a wonderful idea," they said as they saw the kittens. "Let's do it!"

"Sometimes it pays to have a twin sister," said James.

Now have children turn to page 2 and read the directions at the top of the page. Then say: *Answer questions 1–3 on page 2. Read each question carefully. To answer a question, fill in the oval next to the answer you have chosen. Mark only one oval for each question. Make your marks dark and neat. Stop when you reach the stop sign on the bottom of page 2. When you have finished, put down your pencils and look at me. You may begin now.*

Have children answer questions 1 through 3 and stop on page 2.

Reading Comprehension; Vocabulary Strategies; Literary Elements; Text Features and Study Skills; Grammar, Mechanics, and Usage, pages 3–15

Have children turn to page 3. Say: *You will now answer some multiple-choice and short-answer questions. Read all of the selections and questions carefully. You will see that the paragraphs in the reading selections and the lines in the poem are numbered. There also is a number before each sentence in the passage*

© Macmillan/McGraw-Hill

on page 14. These numbers will help you find the sentence or sentences you will need to answer the questions that follow. For each multiple-choice question, read all four answer choices. To answer a multiple-choice question, fill in the oval next to the answer you have chosen. Mark only one oval for each question. Make your marks dark and neat. For each short-answer question, write your answer on the lines provided on the page. Stop when you reach the stop signs and wait for me to tell you to go on. When you have finished, put down your pencils and look at me. You may begin now.

Have children answer questions 4 through 24 and stop on page 15.

Phonics,
pages 16–17

Have children turn to page 16. Say: *I will say the name of each picture. After I say the name, read the four answer choices. Fill in the oval next to the word that names the picture. Mark your answers very carefully and make your marks dark and neat. Are there any questions?*

Respond to any questions.

Say: *Look at Number 25. I will say the name of the picture now. "Kitten." "Kitten." Read the four answer choices and fill in the oval next to the word "Kitten."*

Pause for children to mark their answers.

Say: *We will continue in the same way.*

Number 26: Spider

Number 27: Puzzle

Say: *You will now answer some more multiple-choice Phonics questions. Read each question carefully. For each multiple-choice question, read all four answer choices. Then fill in the oval next to the answer you have chosen.*

Have children answer Numbers 28 to 30 and stop on page 17.

Writing,
pages 18–21

Have children turn to pages 18–19. Say: *Look at the writing prompt on page 18. It is followed by planning page 19. Use this blank page to plan your composition. You may want to make notes to decide what to write. You may want to make a web to put your ideas in an order that makes sense. You may want to write a rough draft. Remember that the more planning you do, the clearer your composition will be.*

Have children turn to pages 20–21. Say: *When you are ready to write your composition, be sure to write on answer document pages 20 and 21, which are the two pages with lines. Your composition does not have to completely fill these two lined pages, but it must not be longer than the two pages.*

Make sure children know what they are expected to do.

Say: *When you have finished writing, put down your pencil and look at me. You may begin writing now.*

© Macmillan/McGraw-Hill

Student Name _____

Date _____

Unit Assessment

TESTED SKILLS AND STRATEGIES

- Listening Comprehension
- Reading Comprehension
- Vocabulary Strategies
- Literary Elements
- Text Features and Study Skills
- Grammar, Mechanics, and Usage
- Phonics
- Writing

Macmillan/McGraw-Hill

DIRECTIONS

Listen as your teacher reads the selection. Then read each question. Decide which is the best answer to each question. Mark the space for the answer you have chosen.

1 When James complains about being a twin, Jennie is —

- **A** very angry
- **B** scared
- **C** not too upset
- **D** thrilled

2 What does James do just before he runs out of the house?

- **A** Sits in the yard
- **B** Looks at kittens in the box
- **C** Goes inside to get Jennie
- **D** Complains about having a twin

3 Why does James say, "Sometimes it pays to have a twin sister?"

- **A** Jennie is always nice to him.
- **B** He likes to share his birthday.
- **C** Jennie understands him.
- **D** Now both kittens can live with them.

Page 2

STOP

Read each selection. Then read each question that follows that selection. Decide which is the best answer to each question. Mark the space for the answer you have chosen. Write your answers to questions 8 and 14.

Charlie's Blue Bag

1   Charlie and his big brother Tom sat on an enormous rock. They had been walking for a long time that morning, and Charlie was happy to stop.

2   Soon they were ready to move on. Tom reached out and started to grab Charlie's blue bag. "Would you like me to help carry this for a while?" he asked.

3   "No, I can carry it," answered Charlie.

4   Tom and Charlie kept walking. The sun was high in the sky. They were still far from Uncle Mac's camp when it was time for lunch. They would not get there for a while. Tom's stomach rumbled.

5   Tom said, "I wish we had some lunch to eat right now." Tom had thought they would be at Uncle Mac's camp already.

GO ON

© Macmillan/McGraw-Hill

6   "Look what I have," said Charlie. He <u>opened</u> his blue bag and pulled out crackers, peanut butter, and oranges. "We can eat right here," said Charlie. Next, he took a bottle of water out from his blue bag. Last, he pulled out a thin blanket. "We can use this picnic blanket, too," Charlie said.

7   Tom said, "Bringing that blue bag was a great idea. Now we can rest our feet and eat lunch. I think I'd better get a bag like that for our next trip."

8   Charlie smiled happily and zipped up his blue bag. They laid down the blanket in a shady spot and started to eat.

---

4 Look at the chart.

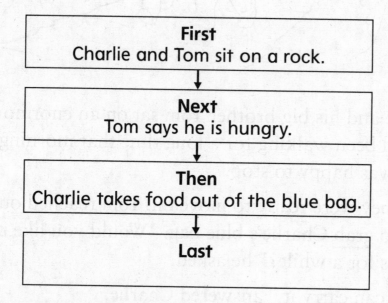

First
Charlie and Tom sit on a rock.

↓

Next
Tom says he is hungry.

↓

Then
Charlie takes food out of the blue bag.

↓

Last

Which of these goes in the *Last* box?

   (A) Tom and Charlie feel tired.

   (B) Tom and Charlie head to Uncle Mac's.

   (C) Tom and Charlie eat lunch.

   (D) Tom pulls out a picnic blanket.

Page 4

5 Which words help you understand the meaning of <u>grab</u> in paragraph 2?

- **(A)** *happy to stop*
- **(B)** *ready to move on*
- **(C)** *Charlie's blue bag*
- **(D)** *Tom reached out*

6 What is the base word for <u>opened</u> in paragraph 6?

- **(A)** open
- **(B)** opening
- **(C)** pen
- **(D)** opens

7 In paragraph 8, Charlie smiles happily because —

- **(A)** he likes to sit on a rock
- **(B)** it is a warm, sunny day
- **(C)** he feels proud that Tom liked his idea
- **(D)** the boys have a gift for Uncle Mac

8 What happens in the story after Tom says that he wished they had lunch to eat? Support your answer with details from the story.

_____

_____

_____

GO ON

© Macmillan/McGraw-Hill

Barack Obama

1   What do you want to be when you grow up? When Barack Obama was in elementary school, he wrote that he wanted to be president.

2   Barack Obama grew up in Hawaii. He lived with his mother and his grandparents. His friends called him Barry. When he was six years old, Barack and his family moved to a country called Indonesia.

3   A few years <u>later</u>, Barack's family moved back to Hawaii. Barack played basketball on his high school's team. Then he went away to college and later to law school.

4   Barack Obama met his wife Michelle in Chicago. They were both lawyers. They have two children, Malia and Sasha.

5   Barack Obama wanted to <u>help</u> other people, so he worked in his community in Chicago. Later, he became a U.S. senator and made laws to help the people of Illinois. He also wrote books about his childhood and beliefs.

6 | Barack Obama was nominated to run for President in 2008. Many people were excited. He won the election on November 4, 2008. He became the first African American president of the United States. He <u>achieved</u> the goal he wrote about when he was young!

9 Which is the best summary of paragraph 2?

(A) Barack Obama's friends called him Barry.

(B) Barack Obama lived with his grandparents.

(C) Barack Obama played basketball on his school's team.

(D) Barack Obama grew up in Hawaii and Indonesia.

10 What is the base word of <u>later</u> in paragraph 3?

(A) lately

(B) lat

(C) late

(D) last

11 From this article you can tell that Barack Obama —

(A) likes Indonesia

(B) has accomplished many things

(C) has never traveled

(D) went to law school in Chicago

GO ON ➡

12 What word from a thesaurus has almost the same meaning as <u>help</u> in paragraph 5?

(A) Assist

(B) Hurt

(C) Meet

(D) Respect

13 What word helps you understand the meaning of <u>achieved</u> in paragraph 6?

(A) *goal*

(B) *young*

(C) *wrote*

(D) *President*

14 Write a summary of paragraphs 5 and 6 of "Barack Obama." Support your answer with details from the article.

_____

_____

_____

_____

DIRECTIONS

Read the poem. Then read each question that follows the poem. Decide which is the best answer to each question. Mark the space for the answer you have chosen.

The Tree and Me

1   One day I sat beside a tree.
2   The tree sang a song to me.
3   Its song was sweet and made me smile.
4   I said I would just sit a while

5   Plip plop! Bop! I heard a sound.
6   I found a lump all big and round.
7   The tree was dropping nuts on me.
8   I ran as quickly as can be!

Page 9

15 Which word is an example of onomatopoeia?

    (A) *lump*

    (B) *dropping*

    (C) *plop*

    (D) *sound*

16 Which words from the poem rhyme?

    (A) *beside* and *while*

    (B) *nuts* and *lump*

    (C) *sound* and *round*

    (D) *sang* and *song*

© Macmillan/McGraw-Hill

STOP

Student Name _____

DIRECTIONS
Decide which is the best answer to each question. Mark the space for the answer you have chosen.

17 Look at the diagram.

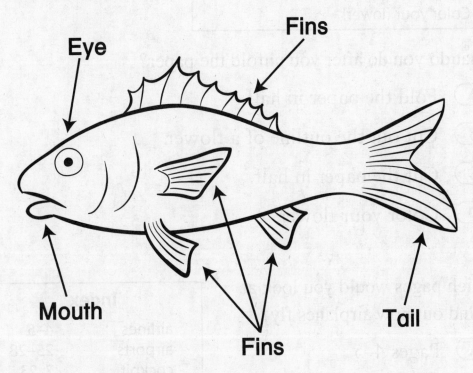

The diagram and the labels show —

(A) what fish eat

(B) where fish live

(C) how fish swim

(D) body parts of a fish

Page 11

18 Read the directions.

> **Paper Flower**
>
> 1. Fold a piece of paper in half.
> 2. Cut out the outline of half of a flower.
> 3. Unfold the paper.
> 4. Color your flower!

What do you do after you unfold the paper?

A Fold the paper in half.

B Cut out the outline of a flower.

C Cut the paper in half.

D Color your flower.

19 Which pages would you look at to find out how airplanes fly?

A Pages 4–5

B Pages 26–27

C Pages 17–19

D Pages 25–28

Index	
airlines	4–5
airports	25–28
cockpit	7, 23
engine	17–19
history	10–15
pilot	6, 11, 17
runways	26–27
wings	20

GO ON ▶

20 Look at the encyclopedia page.

Wolves

Wolves

Wolves are a type of mammal. They are the largest member of the dog family. They can be found in some parts of the United States.

Kinds of Wolves

There are many kinds of wolves. The gray wolf is the most common wolf in the United States. It is the largest wolf and can live in many environments. It might be gray, black, brown, or white. The red wolf is red in color and smaller than the gray wolf. It lives in the southeastern Unites States. The arctic wolf is a subspecies of the gray wolf. It is all white and lives in cold, snowy lands. Its white fur helps it to blend in with the snow.

Gray Wolf

Wolf Packs

Wolves usually live in groups known as packs. Most wolf packs consist of a father, a mother, and their children. Some packs have more members. These packs are usually led by the strongest male and female members, known as the alpha male and female.

The headings tell you —

A what page you are on

B what the sections are about

C when the article was written

D who wrote the article

STOP

© Macmillan/McGraw-Hill

DIRECTIONS
Read the introduction and the passage that follows. Then read each question and fill in the correct answer.

Luis wrote this story about a bird song. He wants you to review his story. As you read, think about the corrections and improvements Luis should make. Then answer the questions that follow.

Listen!

(1) "Listen to our song! cry the birds. (2) They sing a Song that is long and beautiful. (3) Never have me heard such a song! (4) When it is finished, they flies away into the blue, blue sky.

GO ON

© Macmillan/McGraw-Hill

21 What change, if any, should be made in sentence 1?

- **A** Change the period to a comma
- **B** Add a quotation mark after *song!*
- **C** Change *our* to **we**
- **D** Make no change

22 What is the **BEST** way to rewrite sentence 2?

- **A** They sing a song that is Long and Beautiful.
- **B** They sing a song that is long and beautiful.
- **C** they sing a Song that is long and beautiful.
- **D** they sing a song that is long and beautiful.

23 What change, if any, should be made in sentence 3?

- **A** Change *have* to **having**
- **B** Change the exclamation point to a question mark
- **C** Change *me* to **I**
- **D** Make no change

24 What is the **BEST** way to rewrite sentence 4?

- **A** When it is finished, they fly away into the blue, blue sky.
- **B** When it be finished, they flies away into the blue, blue sky.
- **C** When it is finish, they flies away into the blue, blue sky.
- **D** When it is finished, they flying away into the blue, blue sky.

STOP

DIRECTIONS
Mark the space for the word that names the picture.

25

(A) Kidding

(B) Kitten

(C) Bitten

(D) Care

26

(A) Spies

(B) Spinning

(C) Spider

(D) Spilled

27

(A) Pull

(B) Fizzle

(C) Puddle

(D) Puzzle

28 Which word has closed syllables?

(A) Lazy

(B) Pony

(C) Mitten

(D) Tiger

29 Which word has open syllables?

(A) Basket

(B) Knotted

(C) Napkin

(D) Baby

30 Which word has a consonant + *le* syllable as the second syllable?

(A) Candy

(B) Candle

(C) Letter

(D) Leaf

STOP

WRITTEN COMPOSITION

Write a story about how you
solved a problem at school.

The information in the box below will help you remember what you should think
about when you write your composition.

REMEMBER TO –

- write about how you solved a problem at school

- make sure that every sentence you write helps
  the reader understand your composition

- include enough details to help the reader
  clearly understand what you are saying

- use correct spelling, capitalization, punctuation,
  grammar, and sentences

© Macmillan/McGraw-Hill

Page 18

Student Name _____

```
┌─────────────────────────────────────────────┐
│          USE THIS PREWRITING PAGE TO          │
│          PLAN YOUR COMPOSITION                │
└─────────────────────────────────────────────┘
```

```
┌─────────────────────────────────────────────┐
│  MAKE SURE THAT YOU WRITE YOUR COMPOSITION ON │
│         THE LINES ON PAGES 20-21              │
└─────────────────────────────────────────────┘
```

Answer Document

_____

_____

_____

_____

_____

_____

_____

_____

Unit Assessment

Answer Document

_____

_____

_____

_____

_____

_____

_____

_____

_____

Student Name_____

Grade 2 • Unit 5
Student Evaluation Chart

Tested Skills	Number Correct	Percent Correct
Listening Comprehension: *Make Inferences, 1, 3; Sequence of Events, 2*	/3	%
Reading Comprehension: *Sequence of Events, 4; Make Inferences, 7; Summarize, 9; Draw Conclusions, 11*	/4	%
Short answer: *Sequence of Events, 8; Summarize, 14*	/6	%
Vocabulary Strategies: *Context Clues, 5, 13; Word Parts: Base Words, 6, 10; Thesaurus, 12*	/5	%
Literary Elements: *Onomatopoeia, 15; Rhyme, 16*	/2	%
Text Features and Study Skills: *Diagrams and Labels, 17; Written Directions, 18; Narrow a Topic for Research, 19; Encyclopedia, 20*	/4	%
Grammar, Mechanics, and Usage: *Quotation Marks, 21; Capitalization, 22; Pronoun I, 23; Pronoun-Verb Agreement, 24*	/4	%
Phonics: *Closed Syllables, 25, 28; Open Syllables, 26, 29; Consonant + le Syllables, 27, 30*	/6	%
Writing: *Realistic Fiction*	/4	%
Total Unit Test Score	/38	%

This Unit Assessment is designed to measure your children's mastery of the skills taught in the unit. The test assesses all of the following areas:

- Listening Comprehension
- Reading Comprehension
- Vocabulary Strategies
- Literary Elements
- Text Features and Study Skills
- Grammar, Mechanics, and Usage
- Phonics
- Writing

Listening Comprehension, page 2

Say: *Listen while I read this story to you. You will be asked to answer three multiple-choice questions based on this story. Listen carefully. We will begin now.*

The Alaska State Flag

Did you know that a thirteen-year-old boy came up with the Alaska state flag? A long time ago, Alaska did not have a flag. So, a contest was held for seventh graders in Alaska. Students were asked to draw pictures of a new state flag.

Alaskan students went into action. One student drew a polar bear on an iceberg. Another student drew a polar bear on top of a globe. Some drew pictures about fishing. Over 100 drawings were entered in the contest. They all showed something special about Alaska.

Benny Benson put his imagination to work. He drew a flag that was mostly blue. The blue color stood for the Alaskan sky and a blue flower called the forget-me-not. Benny drew a group of stars called the Big Dipper on his flag. He drew the North Star because Alaska is a state that is far north.

Benny's flag won! Benny's flag became the flag for the state of Alaska. It still is today!

Now have children turn to page 2 and read the directions at the top of the page. Then say: *Answer questions 1–3 on page 2. Read each question carefully. To answer a question, fill in the oval next to the answer you have chosen. Mark only one oval for each question. Make your marks dark and neat. Stop when you reach the stop sign on the bottom of page 2. When you have finished, put down your pencils and look at me. You may begin now.*

Have children answer questions 1 through 3 and stop on page 2.

Reading Comprehension; Vocabulary Strategies; Literary Elements; Text Features and Study Skills; Grammar, Mechanics, and Usage, pages 3–15

Have children turn to page 3. Say: *You will now answer some multiple-choice and short-answer questions. Read all of the selections and questions carefully. You will see that the paragraphs in the reading selections and the lines in the poem are numbered. There also is a number before each sentence in the passage on page 14. These numbers will help you find the sentence or sentences you will need to answer the questions that follow. For each multiple-choice question, read all four answer* choices. To answer a multiple-choice question, fill in the oval next to the answer you have chosen. Mark only one oval for each question. Make your marks dark and neat. For each short-answer question, write your answer on the lines provided on the page. Stop when you reach the stop signs and wait for me to tell you to go on. When you have finished, put down your pencils and look at me. You may begin now.*

Have children answer questions 4 through 24 and stop on page 15.

Phonics,
pages 16–17

Have children turn to page 16. Say: *I will say the name of each picture. After I say the name, read the four answer choices. Fill in the oval next to the word that names the picture. Mark your answers very carefully and make your marks dark and neat. Are there any questions?*

Respond to any questions.

Say: *Look at Number 25. I will say the name of the picture now. "Birdcage." "Birdcage." Read the four answer choices and fill in the oval next to the word "Birdcage."*

Pause for children to mark their answers.

Say: *We will continue in the same way.*

Number 26: Seat belt

Number 27: Apple

Say: *You will now answer some more multiple-choice Phonics questions. Read each question carefully. For each multiple-choice question, read all four answer choices. Then fill in the oval next to the answer you have chosen.*

Have children answer Numbers 28 to 30 and stop on page 17.

Writing,

pages 18–21

Have children turn to pages 18–19. Say: *Look at the writing prompt on page 18. It is followed by planning page 19. Use this blank page to plan your composition. You may want to make notes to decide what to write. You may want to make a web to put your ideas in an order that makes sense. You may want to write a rough draft. Remember that the more planning you do, the clearer your composition will be.*

Have children turn to pages 20–21. Say: *When you are ready to write your composition, be sure to write on answer document pages 20 and 21, which are the two pages with lines. Your composition does not have to completely fill these two lined pages, but it must not be longer than the two pages.*

Make sure children know what they are expected to do.

Say: *When you have finished writing, put down your pencil and look at me. You may begin writing now.*

Student Name _____

Date _____

Unit
Assessment
TESTED SKILLS AND STRATEGIES

- Listening Comprehension
- Reading Comprehension
- Vocabulary Strategies
- Literary Elements
- Text Features and Study Skills
- Grammar, Mechanics, and Usage
- Phonics
- Writing

Macmillan/McGraw-Hill

DIRECTIONS

Listen as your teacher reads the selection. Then read each question. Decide which is the best answer to each question. Mark the space for the answer you have chosen.

1 The author wrote this article to —

(A) persuade students to enter the contest

(B) describe how the Alaska state flag came to be

(C) explain why a state flag is important

(D) show what is special about Alaska

2 All of the flags were alike because they —

(A) showed something special about Alaska

(B) had mostly blue backgrounds

(C) contained polar bears

(D) are still the state flag for Alaska

3 What was the effect of Benny's flag winning the contest?

(A) Some students drew pictures about fishing.

(B) One student drew a polar bear on an iceberg.

(C) Alaska did not have a state flag.

(D) It became the state flag for Alaska.

© Macmillan/McGraw-Hill

Page 2

STOP

DIRECTIONS

Read each selection. Then read each question that follows that selection. Decide which is the best answer to each question. Mark the space for the answer you have chosen. Write your answers to questions 8 and 14.

A Fun Indoor Game

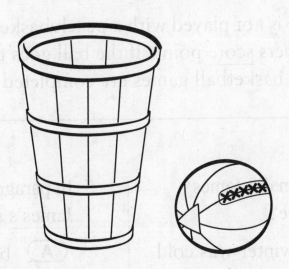

1   Winters in Massachusetts are cold and wet. James Naismith wanted to find a game to play inside during winter. He needed a game that could be played indoors in a small space. James decided to make up a new game.

2   James hung peach baskets on either side of a room. He got a soccer ball. He made a list of rules. James invented a new game. It was called basketball.

3   To play <u>James's</u> game, players could not run with the ball. They could throw it to each other but not hit it with a fist. Players got a point if the soccer ball went into the basket and stayed there. The game was played in two halves.

GO ON

4   James saw his game grow. Soon people all over the world enjoyed playing it.

5   Today basketball is played with a ball that bounces more than a soccer ball. Players can bounce the ball as they run. They still cannot run holding the ball.

6   The game is not played with a peach basket. It is played with a hoop. Players <u>score</u> points if the ball goes through the hoop. Today most basketball games are completed in four quarters.

4 What problem did James Naismith have?

   Ⓐ The winter was cold and wet.

   Ⓑ He had a soccer ball to play with.

   Ⓒ He needed a game to play inside during winter.

   Ⓓ He needed a game to play with peach baskets.

5 In paragraph 3, the word James's means —

   Ⓐ belongs to James

   Ⓑ taken from James

   Ⓒ like James

   Ⓓ people named James

© Macmillan/McGraw-Hill

Page 4

GO ON ▶

6 Today basketball is played differently because —

   A players can run with the ball

   B games are played in two halves

   C it is not played with a peach basket

   D it is played with a soccer ball

7 Which word would you find listed in a dictionary as the meaning of <u>score</u> in paragraph 6?

   A Lose

   B Scratch

   C Gain

   D Run

8 Why did James invent his new game? Explain your answer and support it with details from the article.

_____

_____

_____

_____

GO ON

Page 5

Waiting for Springtime

1   Lamb was tired of the cold weather. "The snow makes my feet cold," he said to Goat.

2   "Winter is almost <u>finished</u>. <u>Springtime</u> will be here soon," said Goat.

3   "I do not want to wait for springtime," Lamb said. "I want to solve my problem now." Lamb looked for something to keep his feet warm. He found some rocks. "Can the rocks keep my feet warm?" he asked Goat.

4   "No," said Goat.

5   Lamb looked for something else to keep his feet warm. He found some pine cones. "Can the pine cones keep my feet warm?" he asked Goat.

6   "No," said Goat.

7   Lamb looked for something else to keep his feet warm. He found some <u>branches</u> of pine needles. "Can the pine needles keep my feet warm?" he asked Goat.

8   "Yes," said Goat.

Page 6

GO ON ➡

9   Lamb and Goat tied the pine needles together and made a pair of socks. Lamb put the socks on his feet. Lamb walked into the snow. His feet were warm. "Now my feet are not cold!" said Lamb.

10   The next day Lamb put the pine-needle socks around his feet and went out to the field. The snow that had covered the ground was gone. Lamb heard a baby bird singing in its nest. He saw a bee flying around some bright flowers. "This is springtime!" said Goat.

11   Lamb was not happy. "My feet are too warm," he told Goat. "When will it be winter?"

---

9 Look at the chart.

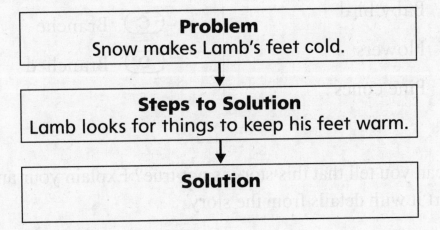

Problem
Snow makes Lamb's feet cold.

↓

Steps to Solution
Lamb looks for things to keep his feet warm.

↓

Solution

Which of these goes in the *Solution* box?

  A Lamb finds some rocks.

  B Lamb finds some pine cones.

  C Lamb makes pine-needle socks.

  D Lamb makes rock socks.

10 The base word for <u>finished</u> in paragraph 2 is —

 (A) finish

 (B) fish

 (C) finishing

 (D) fishes

11 What does Lamb find after he finds rocks but before he finds pine needles?

 (A) Snow

 (B) Baby bird

 (C) Flowers

 (D) Pine cones

12 What is the meaning of <u>springtime</u> in paragraph 2?

 (A) a snowy time

 (B) the season before winter

 (C) the season after winter

 (D) a cold time

13 What is the base word for <u>branches</u> in paragraph 7?

 (A) Bran

 (B) Branch

 (C) Branche

 (D) Branched

14 How can you tell that this story is not true? Explain your answer and support it with details from the story.

_____

_____

_____

GO ON

DIRECTIONS

Read the poem. Then read each question that follows the poem. Decide which is the best answer to each question. Mark the space for the answer you have chosen.

The Purple Cow

1   I never saw a purple cow,
2   I never hope to see one,
3   But I can tell you, anyhow,
4   I'd rather see than be one! Moo!

5   I never saw a polka-dot goat
6   I never hope to see one,
7   But I'll tell you, again I quote,
8   I'd rather see than be one! Meeh!

9   I never saw a striped chicken,
10   I never hope to see one,
11   But I can tell you, once again,
12   I'd rather see than be one! Cluck!

GO ON ➡

Page 9

Unit Assessment

© Macmillan/McGraw-Hill

15 Which words are repeated in this poem?

    (A) *a purple cow*

    (B) *Cluck!*

    (C) *I never saw*

    (D) *again I quote*

16 The poet uses the words *purple*, *polka-dot*, and *striped* to —

    (A) show that the animals are unusual

    (B) describe animals he or she saw

    (C) use rhyming words

    (D) use onomatopoeia

STOP

DIRECTIONS

Decide which is the best answer to each question. Mark the space for the answer you have chosen.

Use the chart to answer questions 17 and 18.

The Great Lakes		
Lake	State It Borders	Size
Lake Ontario	New York	Smallest
Lake Erie	New York, Michigan, Ohio, Pennsylvania	Second in size
Lake Michigan	Michigan, Wisconsin, Illinois, Indiana	Third in size
Lake Huron	Michigan	Fourth in size
Lake Superior	Michigan, Wisconsin, Minnesota	Largest

17 Lake Huron is bordered by —

- (A) New York
- (B) Michigan
- (C) Wisconsin
- (D) Pennsylvania

18 Which lake is the largest?

- (A) Lake Ontario
- (B) Lake Erie
- (C) Lake Michigan
- (D) Lake Superior

GO ON

Use the interview to answer questions 19 and 20.

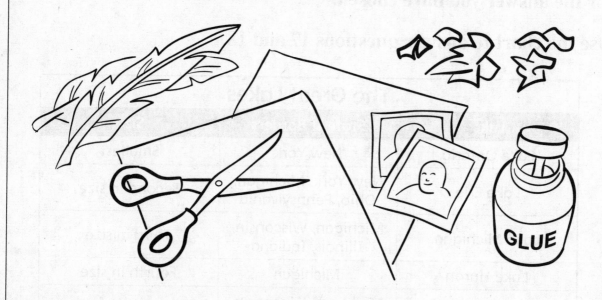

Interview with an Artist

Q: You make collage art. What is a collage?

A: A collage is a picture made by sticking different
materials onto a flat board.

Q: Where do you get ideas for a collage?

A: I get ideas from things I find, like feathers and scraps
of trash. I also get ideas from other collages.

Q: Why do you make collages?

A: I make collages because they are fun.
I like putting different things together to make
something new.

Page 12

GO ON ▶

19 One thing that gives this artist ideas is —

    A glue

    B trash

    C boards

    D scissors

20 The **Q:** tells you —

    A that this is the question

    B to be quiet now

    C to read quickly

    D that the artist's name starts with *Q*

STOP

Read the introduction and the passage that follows. Then read each question and fill in the correct answer.

Paul wrote this story about feeding ducks. He wants you to review his story. As you read, think about the corrections and improvements Paul should make. Then answer the questions that follow.

Feeding the Ducks

(1) Dana and her mother fed the ducks. (2) Of all ducks, one was speckled. (3) The speckled duck was the hungry. (4) The speckled duck ate more than the rest. (5) That duck ate its food quickly. (6) Then it came back for more. (7) The duck quacked at dana before it swam away.

21 What is the **BEST** way to rewrite sentence 2?

(A) Of all duck, one was speckled.

(B) Of all the ducks, one was speckled.

(C) Of all ducks, one was a speckled.

(D) Of all ducks, an one was speckled.

22 What change, if any, should be made to sentence 3?

(A) Change *duck* to Duck

(B) Change *hungry* to hungriest

(C) Add a comma after *speckled*

(D) Make no change

23 What change, if any, should be made to sentence 5?

(A) Insert a comma after *food*

(B) Change *its* to it,s

(C) Change *quickly* to quick

(D) Make no change

24 What is the **BEST** way to rewrite sentence 7?

(A) the duck quacked at dana before it swam away.

(B) The Duck quacked at dana before It swam away.

(C) The Duck quacked at Dana before it swam away.

(D) The duck quacked at Dana before it swam away.

STOP

DIRECTIONS
Mark the space for the word that names the picture.

25

    (A) Birthday

    (B) Caving

    (C) Bird

    (D) Birdcage

26

    (A) Belt

    (B) Seat belt

    (C) Sailboat

    (D) Sealing

27

    (A) Opal

    (B) Pile

    (C) Apply

    (D) Apple

© Macmillan/McGraw-Hill

28 Which word has a vowel-digraph syllable?

(A) Dancing

(B) Settle

(C) Mountain

(D) Biggest

29 Which word has a final *e* syllable?

(A) Feather

(B) Kitchen

(C) Inflate

(D) Friendly

30 Which word has an *r*-controlled vowel syllable?

(A) Highway

(B) Circle

(C) Between

(D) Reaches

STOP

Page 17

WRITTEN COMPOSITION

> Write an article that tells how two games are alike and different.

The information in the box below will help you remember what you should think about when you write your composition.

REMEMBER TO –

- write about how two games are alike and different

- make sure that every sentence you write helps the reader understand your composition

- include enough details to help the reader clearly understand what you are saying

- use correct spelling, capitalization, punctuation, grammar, and sentences

Page 18

USE THIS PREWRITING PAGE TO
PLAN YOUR COMPOSITION

MAKE SURE THAT YOU WRITE YOUR COMPOSITION ON
THE LINES ON PAGES 20-21

Answer Document

_____

_____

_____

_____

_____

_____

_____

_____

_____

Answer Document

_____

_____

_____

_____

_____

_____

_____

_____

_____

_____

Page 21

Student Name _____

Grade 2 • Unit 6
Student Evaluation Chart

Tested Skills	Number Correct	Percent Correct
Listening Comprehension: *Author's Purpose, 1; Compare and Contrast, 2; Cause and Effect, 3*	/3	%
Reading Comprehension: *Problem and Solution, 4; Compare and Contrast, 6; Problem and Solution, 9; Sequence of Events, 11*	/4	%
Short answer: *Cause and Effect, 8; Fantasy Versus Reality, 14*	/6	%
Vocabulary Strategies: *Context Clues: Possessive Nouns, 5; Dictionary: Multiple-Meaning Words, 7; Word Parts: Base Words, 10; Word Parts: Compound Words, 12; Word Parts: Inflectional Nouns, 13*	/5	%
Literary Elements: *Repetition, 15; Word Choice, 16*	/2	%
Text Features and Study Skills: *Charts, 17, 18; Interview, 19; Using Text Features, 20*	/4	%
Grammar, Mechanics, and Usage: *Use the Articles* a, an, *and* the, *21; Adjectives That Compare, 22; Adverbs, 23; Proper Nouns, 24*	/4	%
Phonics: *r-Controlled Syllables, 25, 30; Vowel-Digraph Syllables, 26, 28; Consonant +* le *Syllables, 27; Final* e *Syllables, 29*	/6	%
Writing: *Compare and Contrast*	/4	%
Total Unit Test Score	/38	%

© Macmillan/McGraw-Hill

STUDENT ANSWER SHEET

UNIT ASSESSMENT

S-1 Ⓐ Ⓑ Ⓒ Ⓓ   S-3 Ⓐ Ⓑ Ⓒ Ⓓ
S-2 Ⓐ Ⓑ Ⓒ Ⓓ   S-4 Ⓐ Ⓑ Ⓒ Ⓓ

1 Ⓐ Ⓑ Ⓒ Ⓓ   11 Ⓐ Ⓑ Ⓒ Ⓓ   21 Ⓐ Ⓑ Ⓒ Ⓓ
2 Ⓐ Ⓑ Ⓒ Ⓓ   12 Ⓐ Ⓑ Ⓒ Ⓓ   22 Ⓐ Ⓑ Ⓒ Ⓓ
3 Ⓐ Ⓑ Ⓒ Ⓓ   13 Ⓐ Ⓑ Ⓒ Ⓓ   23 Ⓐ Ⓑ Ⓒ Ⓓ
4 Ⓐ Ⓑ Ⓒ Ⓓ   14 Write answer   24 Ⓐ Ⓑ Ⓒ Ⓓ
5 Ⓐ Ⓑ Ⓒ Ⓓ   15 Ⓐ Ⓑ Ⓒ Ⓓ   25 Ⓐ Ⓑ Ⓒ Ⓓ
6 Ⓐ Ⓑ Ⓒ Ⓓ   16 Ⓐ Ⓑ Ⓒ Ⓓ   26 Ⓐ Ⓑ Ⓒ Ⓓ
7 Ⓐ Ⓑ Ⓒ Ⓓ   17 Ⓐ Ⓑ Ⓒ Ⓓ   27 Ⓐ Ⓑ Ⓒ Ⓓ
8 Write answer   18 Ⓐ Ⓑ Ⓒ Ⓓ   28 Ⓐ Ⓑ Ⓒ Ⓓ
9 Ⓐ Ⓑ Ⓒ Ⓓ   19 Ⓐ Ⓑ Ⓒ Ⓓ   29 Ⓐ Ⓑ Ⓒ Ⓓ
10 Ⓐ Ⓑ Ⓒ Ⓓ   20 Ⓐ Ⓑ Ⓒ Ⓓ   30 Ⓐ Ⓑ Ⓒ Ⓓ

STOP

STUDENT ANSWER SHEET

8 _____

_____

_____

_____

14 _____

_____

_____

_____

       Unit Assessment

Short-Answer Reading Rubric

Use the rubric below to score the short-answer items in the tests.

Score	Description
3	An **exemplary** response gives an interesting and detailed response strongly supported by text evidence.
2	A **sufficient** response gives a clear and reasonable response supported by text evidence.
1	A **partially sufficient** response gives a reasonable but vague response weakly connected to text evidence.
0	An **insufficient** response does not respond to the question.

Evidence may be specific words from the story or a retelling.

Grade 2 Answer Key

Sample Questions

Question	Answer	Content Focus
S-1	B	Compare and Contrast
S-2	C	Character and Setting
S-3	C	Capitalization and Punctuation
S-4	D	Pronouns: *I, me, we, us*

UNIT 1

Question	Answer	Content Focus
1	B	Character
2	C	Plot
3	A	Character
4	D	Character
5	B	Words Ending in -ed
6	B	Plot
7	D	Prefixes
8	See sample answers	Make/Confirm Predictions
9	B	Main Idea and Details
10	B	Words Ending in -ed
11	D	Main Idea and Details
12	A	Dictionary/ABC Order
13	C	Prefixes

Question	Answer	Content Focus
14	See sample answers	Main Idea and Details
15	A	Rhyme
16	C	Rhythmic Patterns
17	D	Photos and Captions
18	A	Using Parts of a Book
19	B	Bar Graphs
20	C	Bar Graphs
21	B	Sentence Capitalization and Punctuation
22	B	Subjects and Predicates
23	B	Sentence Combining
24	C	Letter Punctuation
25	A	Short o
26	C	Short a
27	A	Short e
28	D	Soft c
29	C	Consonant Digraph sh
30	D	Long o

Sample Answers for Question 8:

3-Point Answer: I predicted that Kim would help Mrs. Neal out to pay for the broken window. I read that Kim did not have enough money to pay for the window but she had a good idea. When I read that Kim and her friends were at Mrs. Neal's house the next day, I knew my prediction was correct.

2-Point Answer: I thought Kim's idea would be to help out Mrs. Neal. She did this because she did not have any money for a window.

1-Point Answer: Kim would help out Mrs. Neal.

Sample Answers for Question 14:

3-Point Answer: Stripes help a tiger to camouflage. Camouflage means to disappear by matching what is around you. A tiger's colored stripes help it match the grass in the jungle. When the tiger is camouflaged, the animals it is hunting can't see it. That makes it a better hunter.

2-Point Answer: A tiger has yellow, orange, red, and black stripes. The stripes match the grass in the jungle. Matching the grass helps the tiger disappear when it is hunting.

1-Point Answer: Stripes help tigers hide in the grass.

UNIT 2

Question	Answer	Content Focus
1	C	Character
2	A	Main Idea and Details
3	B	Cause and Effect
4	D	Main Idea and Details
5	A	Context Clues
6	A	Main Idea and Details
7	A	Context Clues: Multiple-Meaning Words
8	See sample answers	Compare and Contrast
9	A	Character
10	A	Word Parts: Word Families
11	C	Cause and Effect
12	C	Context Clues: Multiple-Meaning Words
13	B	Word Parts: Suffixes
14	See sample answers	Make Inferences
15	D	Rhyme
16	B	Rhythmic Patterns
17	A	Maps
18	A	Time Lines

Unit Assessment

Question	Answer	Content Focus
19	B	Photos and Captions
20	B	Using Parts of a Book
21	B	Possessive Nouns
22	D	Proper Nouns
23	A	Using Commas in a Series
24	A	Plural Nouns
25	D	Consonant blend *tr-*
26	C	Consonant blend *dr-*
27	B	Long *a*, ay
28	B	Long *i*, ie
29	A	Long *o*, ow
30	D	Long *o*, oa

Sample Answers for Question 8:

3-Point Answer: Both pine-cone bird feeders and milk-jug bird feeders are easy to make. You need birdseed and wire to make both. You hang both feeders high in a tree and can watch birds come to eat the birdseed.

2-Point Answer: You can make both pine-cone bird feeders and milk-jug bird feeders. You hang them with wire in a tree and watch the birds.

1-Point Answer: They are both bird feeders you hang in the tree and you can watch the birds.

Sample Answers for Question 14:

3-Point Answer: I think that Laura felt excited about her trip on the zoo train. She did not want to miss the train, so she ran to it. She was fearful when the train went fast but she felt better later. She got to watch animals and see the petting zoo.

2-Point Answer: Laura was excited to go on the zoo train. She was scared when it was fast but then she felt better.

1-Point Answer: Laura was excited to go on the zoo train.

UNIT 3

Question	Answer	Content Focus
1	A	Summarize
2	C	Main Idea and Details
3	D	Author's Purpose
4	B	Cause and Effect
5	D	Context Clues: Multiple-Meaning Words
6	D	Cause and Effect
7	A	Thesaurus
8	See sample answers	Summarize
9	D	Draw Conclusions
10	C	Word Parts: Suffixes
11	A	Author's Purpose
12	A	Thesaurus
13	D	Context Clues
14	See sample answers	Summarize
15	C	Alliteration
16	A	Onomatopoeia
17	D	Bar Graphs
18	A	Bar Graphs

Unit Assessment

Question	Answer	Content Focus
19	C	Choose Research Materials
20	D	Headings
21	C	Abbreviations
22	D	The Verb *have*
23	D	Past-Tense Verbs
24	C	Book Titles
25	D	Silent letters *-mb*
26	D	*r*-Controlled Vowels
27	C	*r*-Controlled Vowels
28	D	*r*-Controlled Vowels
29	D	*r*-Controlled Vowels
30	D	*r*-Controlled Vowels

Sample Answers for Question 8:

3-Point Answer: On Jam Day, Tim's family wakes up early to go to the country. There, they pick blackberries for jam. This year Tim's friend Ray comes along for the first time. Ray surprises everyone by picking blackberries very fast.

2-Point Answer: On Jam Day, they go to the country to pick blackberries. Ray comes along and picks blackberries very fast. He worked very hard.

1-Point Answer: They go to pick blackberries for jam.

Sample Answers for Question 14:

3-Point Answer: Popcorn has been a good snack for a long time. American Indians heated the first popcorn on rocks to eat it. Then the Europeans came to America and learned about popcorn. They ate it as cereal. Popcorn pops only when the seeds are wet inside and they get very hot.

2-Point Answer: Popcorn is a snack. Popcorn has been found in old, old caves. People eat it right off the ear. Seeds without enough water do not pop.

1-Point Answer: People have eaten it as a snack for a long time.

UNIT 4

Question	Answer	Content Focus
1	A	Sequence of Events
2	D	Author's Purpose
3	B	Text Structure: Fiction Versus Nonfiction
4	C	Sequence of Events
5	A	Word Parts: Compound Words
6	D	Main Idea and Details
7	A	Word Parts: Base Words
8	See sample answers	Sequence of Events
9	B	Cause and Effect
10	A	Dictionary: Homophones
11	A	Context Clues
12	D	Word Parts: Compound Words
13	C	Use Illustrations
14	See sample answers	Distinguish Between Fantasy and Reality
15	A	Simile
16	A	Rhyme
17	D	Drop-Down Menus

Question	Answer	Content Focus
18	B	Floor Plan
19	C	Using the Internet
20	D	Written Directions
21	C	Helping Verbs
22	C	Irregular Verbs
23	C	Quotation Marks
24	A	Contractions
25	B	Vowel Diphthong -ow
26	C	Vowel Diphthong -oy
27	D	Vowel Digraph -oo
28	D	Vowel Digraph -aw
29	A	Vowel Digraph -oo
30	A	Vowel Digraph -oo

Sample Answers for Question 8:

3-Point Answer: After a person calls 911, the 911 workers get someone to come to help. Usually paramedics come to help. They come in teams of one or two people. They bring the person to the hospital in an ambulance.

2-Point Answer: After someone calls 911, the paramedics come to help. They bring the person to the hospital in an ambulance.

1-Point Answer: The paramedics take the person to the hospital.

Sample Answers for Question 14:

3-Point Answer: The story is a fantasy. In the story, two elves help a shoemaker and his wife by making shoes. Shoemakers are real, but elves are make-believe creatures that do not exist.

2-Point Answer: The story is a fantasy. There are no such things as elves.

1-Point Answer: The story is not real.

UNIT 5

Question	Answer	Content Focus
1	C	Make Inferences
2	D	Sequence of Events
3	D	Make Inferences
4	C	Sequence of Events
5	D	Context Clues
6	A	Word Parts: Base Words
7	C	Make Inferences
8	See sample answers	Sequence of Events
9	D	Summarize
10	C	Word Parts: Base Words
11	B	Draw Conclusions
12	A	Thesaurus
13	A	Context Clues
14	See sample answers	Summarize
15	C	Onomatopoeia
16	C	Rhyme
17	D	Diagrams and Labels
18	D	Written Directions
19	C	Narrow a Topic for Research

Question	Answer	Content Focus
20	B	Encyclopedia
21	B	Quotation Marks
22	B	Capitalization
23	C	Pronoun *I*
24	A	Pronoun-Verb Agreement
25	B	Closed Syllables
26	C	Open Syllables
27	D	Consonant + *le* Syllables
28	D	Closed Syllables
29	C	Open Syllables
30	B	Consonant + *le* Syllables

Sample Answers for Question 8:

3-Point Answer: After Tom said that he wished they had something to eat, his brother Charlie showed Tom what he had in his blue bag. He had brought crackers, peanut butter, and oranges to eat and water to drink. He had also brought a blanket. The brothers sat on the blanket to have their lunch.

2-Point Answer: Tom's brother Charlie showed him the food and the blanket he had brought in his blue bag. They sat on the blanket to have their lunch.

1-Point Answer: Tom and Charlie had lunch.

Sample Answers for Question 14:

3-Point Answer: Barack Obama wanted to help people. He became a senator and made laws. Then Barack Obama ran for President. He won the election in 2008. He was the first African American President.

2-Point Answer: Barack Obama became a senator. Then he ran for president and won. He is the first African American President.

1-Point Answer: Barack Obama was a senator and then the President.

UNIT 6

Question	Answer	Content Focus
1	B	Author's Purpose
2	A	Compare and Contrast
3	D	Cause and Effect
4	C	Problem and Solution
5	A	Context Clues: Possessive Nouns
6	C	Compare and Contrast
7	C	Dictionary: Multiple-Meaning Words
8	See sample answers	Cause and Effect
9	C	Problem and Solution
10	A	Word Parts: Base Words
11	D	Sequence of Events
12	C	Word Parts: Compound Words
13	B	Word Parts: Inflectional Nouns
14	See sample answers	Fantasy Versus Reality
15	C	Repetition
16	A	Word Choice
17	B	Charts
18	D	Charts

Unit Assessment

Question	Answer	Content Focus
19	B	Interview
20	A	Using Text Features
21	B	Use the Articles *a*, *an*, and *the*
22	B	Adjectives That Compare
23	D	Adverbs
24	D	Proper Nouns
25	D	*r*-Controlled Syllables
26	B	Vowel-Digraph Syllables
27	D	Consonant + *le* Syllables
28	C	Vowel-Digraph Syllables
29	C	Final *e* Syllables
30	B	*r*-Controlled Syllables

Sample Answer for Question 8:

3-Point Answer: James invented his game because he wanted a game to play during winter. Winters in Massachusetts are cold and wet. James wanted a game to play inside in a small space.

2-Point Answer: James invented his game to have something to play indoors during the winter.

1-Point Answer: James wanted a game to play inside.

Sample Answer for Question 14:

3-Point Answer: The story is a fantasy. In the story, the lamb and the goat talk to each other and they make socks. Animals do not talk to each other and they cannot make things like socks.

2-Point Answer: The story is not true. The animals in it talk and make socks. Animals can't do those things.

1-Point Answer: The story is not real because animals can't talk.

WRITING RUBRICS
SCORE POINT 1

EACH COMPOSITION AT THIS SCORE POINT IS AN INEFFECTIVE PRESENTATION OF THE WRITER'S IDEAS.

Focus and Coherence

- Individual paragraphs and/or the entire composition are not focused. The writer may shift abruptly from idea to idea, making it difficult for the reader to understand how the ideas in the composition are related.

- The entire composition has little sense of completeness. The introduction and conclusion, if present, may be perfunctory.

- A large amount of writing may be unrelated and may not contribute to the development or quality of the entire composition. At times, the composition may be only weakly connected to the prompt.

Organization

- The writer's progression of thought between sentences and/or paragraphs is not logical. Occasionally weak progression results from a lack of transitions or from the use of transitions that do not make sense. At other times, the progression of thought is not evident, even if appropriate transitions are present.

- An organizational strategy is not evident. The writer may present ideas randomly, making the composition difficult to follow.

- Wordiness and/or repetition may inhibit the progression of ideas.

Development of Ideas

- The writer presents one or more ideas but provides little development of those ideas.

- The writer presents one or more ideas and makes an attempt to develop them. However, the development is general or vague, making it difficult for the reader to understand the writer's ideas.

- The writer presents only a plot summary of a published piece of writing, movie, or television show.

- The writer leaves out important information, which creates gaps between ideas. These gaps inhibit the reader's understanding of the ideas.

Voice

- The writer does not use language that engages the reader and therefore fails to establish a connection.

- There may be no evidence of the writer's individual voice. The composition does not sound authentic or original. The writer does not express his/her individuality or unique perspective.

Conventions

- There is little evidence in the composition that the writer can correctly apply the English language conventions. Severe and/or frequent errors in spelling, capitalization, punctuation, grammar, usage, and sentence structure may cause the writing to be difficult to read. These errors weaken the composition by causing a lack of fluency.

- The writer may misuse or omit words and phrases, and may frequently include awkward sentences. These weaknesses inhibit the effective communication of ideas.

SCORE POINT 2

EACH COMPOSITION AT THIS SCORE POINT IS A SOMEWHAT EFFECTIVE PRESENTATION OF THE WRITER'S IDEAS.

Focus and Coherence
- Individual paragraphs and/or the entire composition are somewhat focused. The writer may shift quickly from idea to idea, but the reader can easily understand how the ideas in the composition are related.
- The entire composition has some sense of completeness. The writer includes an introduction and conclusion, but they may be superficial.
- Some of the writing may be unrelated and may not contribute to the development or quality of the entire composition.

Organization
- The writer's progression of thought between sentences and/or paragraphs may not always be smooth or logical. Occasionally, the writer should strengthen the progression by including more meaningful transitions; at other times the writer needs to establish stronger links between ideas.
- The organizational strategies the writer chooses do not allow the writer to present ideas effectively.
- Some wordiness and/or repetition may be present, but these weaknesses do not completely inhibit the progression of ideas.

Development of Ideas
- The writer attempts to develop the composition by listing or briefly explaining the ideas. The development remains superficial, preventing the reader's full understanding of the writer's ideas.
- The writer presents one or more ideas and attempts to develop them. There is little evidence of depth of thinking. The development may be mostly general, inconsistent, or contrived.
- The writer may leave out small pieces of information that create minor gaps between ideas. These gaps do not inhibit the reader's understanding of the ideas.

Voice
- There may be moments when the writer uses language that engages the reader, but the writer fails to sustain the connection.
- Individual paragraphs or sections of the composition sound authentic or original, but the writer does not generally express his/her individuality or unique perspective.

Conventions
- Errors in spelling, capitalization, punctuation, grammar, usage, and sentence structure throughout the composition may indicate a limited control of English language conventions. These errors may not cause the writing to be unclear, however they may weaken the overall fluency of the composition.
- The writer may employ simple or inaccurate words and phrases and may write some awkward sentences. These weaknesses inhibit the overall effectiveness of the communication of ideas.

SCORE POINT 3

EACH COMPOSITION AT THIS SCORE POINT IS A GENERALLY EFFECTIVE PRESENTATION OF THE WRITER'S IDEAS.

Focus and Coherence

- Individual paragraphs and the composition are, for the most part, focused. The writer generally shows the distinct relationship between ideas, rarely making sudden shifts from one idea to the next.

- The composition has a sense of completeness. The introduction and conclusion add depth to the composition.

- Most of the writing contributes to the development or quality of the entire composition.

Organization

- The writer's progression of thought between sentences and/or paragraphs is, for the most part, smooth and controlled. Usually, transitions are meaningful, and the links between ideas are logical.

- The organizational strategies the writer chooses are usually effective.

- Wordiness and repetition, if present, are minor problems that do not inhibit the progression of ideas.

Development of Ideas

- The writer attempts to develop all the ideas in the composition. Some ideas may be developed more thoroughly and specifically than others, but the development reflects some depth of thought, allowing the reader to generally understand and appreciate the writer's ideas.

- The writer's presentation of some ideas may be thoughtful. Little evidence exists that the writer has been willing to take compositional risks when developing the topic.

Voice

- The writer uses language that engages the reader and sustains that connection throughout most of the composition.

- In general, the composition sounds authentic and original. The writer usually expresses his/her individuality or unique perspective.

Conventions

- There is evidence that the writer generally demonstrates a good command of spelling, capitalization, punctuation, grammar, usage, and sentence structure. Although there may be minor errors, they create few disruptions in the fluency of the composition.

- The words, phrases, and sentence structures the writer employs are generally appropriate and contribute to the overall effectiveness of the communication of ideas.

SCORE POINT 4

EACH COMPOSITION AT THIS SCORE POINT IS A HIGHLY EFFECTIVE PRESENTATION OF THE WRITER'S IDEAS.

Focus and Coherence

- Individual paragraphs and the entire composition are focused. This sustained focus allows the reader to understand how the ideas included in the composition are related.
- The entire composition has a sense of completeness. The introduction and conclusion add meaningful depth to the composition.
- Most, if not all, of the writing contributes to the development or quality of the entire composition.

Organization

- The writer's progression of thought between sentences and/or paragraphs is smooth and controlled. The writer's use of meaningful transitions and the logical movement from idea to idea strengthen this progression.
- The organizational strategies the writer chooses allow the writer to present ideas clearly and effectively.

Development of Ideas

- The writer's thorough and specific development of each idea creates depth of thought in the composition, allowing the reader to fully understand and appreciate the writer's ideas.
- The writer's presentation of ideas is thoughtful or insightful. The writer may approach the topic from an unusual perspective, use his/her unique experiences or view of the world as a basis for writing, or make interesting connections between ideas. In all these cases, the writer's willingness to take compositional risks improves the quality of the composition.

Voice

- The writer uses language that engages the reader and sustains this connection throughout the composition.
- The composition sounds authentic and original. The writer expresses his/her individuality or unique perspective.

Conventions

- The strength of the conventions contributes to the effectiveness of the composition. The writer demonstrates a consistent command of spelling, capitalization, punctuation, grammar, usage, and sentence structure. When the writer communicates complex ideas through advanced forms of expression, he/she may make minor errors as a result of these compositional risks. These types of errors do not take away from the overall fluency of the composition.
- The words, phrases, and sentence structures the writer uses enhance the effectiveness of the communication of ideas.

Anchor Papers: Student Writing Samples

This section provides sample written responses to the Unit writing prompts, along with comments explaining the scores.

Unit 1: Personal Narrative

Score Point 1

Mr. Luz

Kids liks mr. Luz. Me to. He cleen and kep things neet. Mr. luz does them with school work. Finds things they lost. Everone say sprise. Mr. luz coms to work. Some kids get him somthin nis, it was a ti and soks. Its a sprise.

Focus and Coherence—weak connection to prompt; writer does not give information about something that happened on the way to school; purpose of the composition is vague; lacks focus; no sense of completeness

Organization—progression of thought and details are illogical; lacks transitions; ideas are random

Development of Ideas/Word Choice—very little development of ideas; words may not be used correctly, such as "does them with school work"

Voice—individual voice is not expressed in the writing; writer does not engage the reader; lacks connection

Conventions/Sentence Fluency—little to no command of spelling, capitalization, punctuation, grammar, usage, and sentence structure skills; awkward sentences interfere with the ideas communicated by the writer

Ducks

This was a surpising morning. We are careful when we walk up to school. Because we dont want to step on a harmles duck. Making a nest, the playground was home to a mother duck. That day their were six baby ducks. The ducks they are cute. I saw some ducks in a petting zoo. They somtimes walk to the front of the school.

I went to shcool. Here was the surpise. This time the ducks wouldnt let me in the door! The ducks came from the playground to the front door. When I tried to get in I couldn't. They where garding the school.

Focus and Coherence—writer focuses on describing something that happened on the way to school but shifts quickly from idea to idea; paragraphs are somewhat focused; superficial introduction and conclusion; composition has some sense of completeness

Organization—ineffective organization; writer strays from topic (e.g., I saw some ducks in a petting zoo.); illogical progression of thought; some wordiness and repetition

Development of Ideas/Word Choice—development of ideas is superficial, which limits the reader's understanding of the composition; word choice does not suit purpose

Voice—writer engages the reader but fails to sustain the connection; shows little unique perspective

Conventions/Sentence Fluency— limited command of spelling, capitalization, punctuation, grammar, usage, and sentence structure skills; composition is not fluent; sentences are awkward

A Scary Ride

Mr. Black drives my school bus. He always smiles and says hello when I get on the bus in the morning. All the kids like him. He's a good driver but once day something hapened that was scary.

That day Mr. Black was driving to our school. Out of nowear jumps a deer! Mr. Black stopped the bus fast. Me and the other kids were scared. Mr. Black parked the bus. We looked out the window and saw the deer running a way. We were all okay but Mr. Black called the police just in case.

Focus and Coherence—paragraphs and ideas are focused; introduction and conclusion add depth to the composition; sense of completeness

Organization—progression of thought is generally logical; well-organized with a clear beginning, middle, and end

Development of Ideas/Word Choice—development of ideas shows depth of thought; writer's word choice suits the composition's purpose

Voice—writer uses an authentic and original voice, which engages and sustains a connection with the reader (e.g., Me and the other kids were scared.)

Conventions/Sentence Fluency—good command of spelling, capitalization, punctuation, grammar, usage, and sentence structure skills; writer uses appropriate words and phrases

Scamp

On the way to school one day, I saw a little dog. He walked up to me and he happily waged his tail. I reached down to pet him, and then he licked my hand. He made me smile! He was the cutest dog I ever saw. Sinse he didn't have a collar, I couldn't tell if he belonged to anyone. What now?

I couldn't leave the poor guy on the street, so I picked him up and took him to school. My teacher told me we couldn't keep him in class. I knew that I couldn't take him home because we alredy had a dog. That's when I called my aunt who loves animals. She came right over and picked him up. It was love at first site. She named him Scamp, and now he lives with her. I'm happy because I can visit Scamp when I want to.

Focus and Coherence—composition is focused; writer gives interesting and detailed information about the topic and includes a strong introduction and conclusion

Organization—smooth and logical progression of thought; ideas are presented clearly and effectively

Development of Ideas/Word Choice—writer develops his/her ideas thoroughly; words chosen are precise and enhance the quality of the writing

Voice—authentic and original voice engages the reader (e.g., What now?)

Conventions/Sentence Fluency—consistent command of spelling, capitalization, punctuation, grammar, usage, and sentence structure skills; ideas are communicated effectively

Score Point 1

How farv

How far is good. Its fun. We play al the time. You has to beet the time of an other kid. Like sam got to the wall in 20 secunds. sam is best frend. But maria dos it in 17 secunds.

I like to play out side, we play ever day its fun. Not on rany day.

Focus and Coherence—composition is unfocused; writer shifts from idea to idea; little or no sense of completeness

Organization—writing is disorganized; ideas are presented in a random or haphazard way; lacks transitions

Development of Ideas/Word Choice—ideas are not developed; words are omitted (e.g., sam is best frend.) and not used correctly (e.g., ever day)

Voice—individual voice is not expressed; composition does not sound authentic or original

Conventions/Sentence Fluency—little to no command of spelling, capitalization, punctuation, grammar, usage, and sentence structure skills; awkward sentences interfere with the ideas communicated by the writer

Bucket Ball

Bucket Ball is a game. You start with 6 buckets in a sqare. That's how to do Bucket Ball. There are 12 players. 6 players have to put balls into they're buckets. Then 6 others have to take them out. and the one with the most at the end wins.

But the kids who take out the balls have to go round in a sqare. and they cant turn round. Play outside. I like to play outside best. So summer is my favorite time.

Focus and Coherence—lacks a strong introduction and conclusion; composition is somewhat focused but includes some extraneous thoughts that do not contribute to the development of the composition

Organization—writer omits ideas and does not use transitions; ideas are not presented in an effective and logical order

Development of Ideas/Word Choice—writer presents ideas but does not develop them completely; word choice does not suit purpose

Voice—writer engages the reader but fails to sustain the connection; shows little unique perspective

Conventions/Sentence Fluency—limited command of spelling, capitalization, punctuation, grammar, usage, and sentence structure skills; composition is not fluent; sentences are awkward

Duck, Duck, Goose

It's fun to play duck, duck, goose. We play with 10 kids. First the kids sit down in a circle and face each other. One kid is the picker. Then the picker starts to tap each kid and calling out duck! But the ducks don't move. The picker's job is hardest.

Then the picker calls one kid a goose. The goose gets up and chayses the picker. The picker tries to get to the spot where the goose was sitting. If this happen the goose becomes the picker. The goose tried to tag the picker first. When this happens the goose gets to sit back down. Then the picker starts all over again.

Focus and Coherence—composition is mostly focused and there is a clear relationship between ideas; introduction and conclusion add depth; writer uses details that help contribute to the development of his/her ideas

Organization—ideas are presented in a logical order; writer sequences the steps to the game Duck, Duck, Goose; uses meaningful transitions

Development of Ideas/Word Choice—writer's ideas are developed and show depth of thought; word choice suits the composition's purpose

Voice—composition sounds authentic; writer expresses his/her individual perspective (e.g., The picker's job is hardest.)

Conventions/Sentence Fluency—good command of spelling, capitalization, punctuation, grammar, usage, and sentence structure skills; writer uses appropriate words and phrases

Red Light, Green Light

"Red light, green light" is a great playground game. To play you need at least 3 people. One kid is the stop light. All the other kids stand in a line about 15 feet away. The stop light faces away from the other kids and calls out "Green light." That's when the kids can run to the stop light. At any time, the stop light can face the others and call out "Red light." Then the others must freeze in place. Players who don't stop are out.

The game goes on when the stop light turns back around and says "Green light." The kid who gets far enough to touch the stop light wins. That kid will be the stop light for the next game. If all the kids are out before anyone tuches the stop light, then the stop light wins.

Focus and Coherence—writer gives interesting and detailed information about the topic; strong introduction and conclusion; composition has a sense of completeness

Organization—composition is well-organized; smooth progression from sentence to sentence; ideas are presented clearly and effectively

Development of Ideas/Word Choice—ideas are developed thoroughly using specific details; word choice is precise and enhances the quality of the writing

Voice—writer connects with the reader; composition sounds authentic and original

Conventions/Sentence Fluency—consistent command of spelling, capitalization, punctuation, grammar, usage, and sentence structure skills; ideas are communicated effectively

Unit 3: Expository Writing: Persuasive Letter

Score Point 1

Deer mrs. Johnson, me and Bob go to the spas musem. Planes are cool, they are old, but some is knew to. I go out on sundays with Bob. Have a good time mostly.

Bob didn't have no money. Mom pade, than we got in but Bob say he get few dolars from his dad to pa bak. I like to go agin. Mike.

Focus and Coherence—writing is not focused on topic; purpose is vague

Organization—illogical progression of thoughts; writer presents ideas in a random way without an organizational strategy (e.g., Mike talks about the space museum, planes, and then going places with Bob on Sundays.); composition is difficult to follow

Development of Ideas/Word Choice—little or no development of ideas; words are omitted (e.g., I like to go agin.); words are not used correctly

Voice—an authentic voice is not used; writer does not connect with the reader

Conventions/Sentence Fluency—little to no command of spelling, capitalization, punctuation, grammar, usage, and sentence structure skills; awkward sentences interfere with the ideas communicated by the writer

Score Point 2

Deer Mr. Bates,

The farm is a good place to go for a trip. Espechully if you like animels. I like the baby animels best. Some times I get a bag of food to feed the little goats. You pay for the bag. I didnt like to milk the cow tho. Because it was yucky. I love choklat milk best.

The hay ride was okay. Made me sneeze. Going on the pony ride was fun. Ponys are smaler than horses.

In a few hours, we saw alot of stuff on the tore. On farms they grow food too. I like the pumkins. I picked a pumkin their. They were big. I know everyone wuld like the farm a lot.

Yours, Don Moss

Focus and Coherence—writer focuses on topic but shifts from idea to idea; paragraphs are somewhat focused; superficial introduction and conclusion; composition has some sense of completeness

Organization—ineffective organization; writer strays from topic (e.g., I love choklat milk best.); illogical progression of thought; some wordiness and repetition

Development of Ideas/Word Choice—development of ideas is superficial, which limits the reader's understanding of the composition; small pieces of information are omitted (e.g., Don might have added more details about why he likes baby animals best.)

Voice—writer engages the reader but fails to sustain the connection; shows little unique perspective

Conventions/Sentence Fluency— limited command of spelling, capitalization, punctuation, grammar, usage, and sentence structure skills; composition is not fluent; sentences are awkward

Score Point 3

Dear Mrs. Brown,

I think a trip to the fire station is a great field trip. There are many neat things to see and do. We can take a tour of the stashun. You get to see all the things used in fighting a fire. And reel fire fighters talk to you. They tell you what it takes to do their job.

An importent thing is we can also find out how to keep safe in a fire. A movie shows how to get out of a burning house. Fire fighters tell you what you should do to keep safe. An example is you shoud stay low. This will help you breath. I believe a trip to the fire station will be fun, and will help keep us safe.

Yours truly, Maria Valdez

Focus and Coherence—paragraphs and ideas are focused; introduction and conclusion add depth to the composition; sense of completeness

Organization—progression of thought is generally logical; well-organized

Development of Ideas/Word Choice—development of ideas shows depth of thought; writer uses examples to explain each reason why the fire station is a great field trip; writer's word choice suits the composition's purpose

Voice—writer uses an authentic and original voice, which engages and sustains a connection with the reader

Conventions/Sentence Fluency—good command of spelling, capitalization, punctuation, grammar, usage, and sentence structure skills; writer uses appropriate words and phrases

Unit Assessment

Score Point 4

Dear Ms. Martin,

The South Street Zoo is a special place. I think the class should go there on a field trip. The zoo has all kinds of animals. There is everything from tiny bats to dolfins. The class can get to see the animals we read about in school. It's fun to read about sea lions. But it's better to see the real thing.

Also, there is a lot to do at the zoo. Some kids can have a tug-of-war with an elephant. Others can feed the birds. But all of us can get close to the animals. And all of us will have a good time. This trip is one the class won't forget.

Yours truly, Ben King

Focus and Coherence—writer gives interesting and detailed information about the topic; composition is focused; writer includes a strong introduction and conclusion (e.g., This trip is one the class won't forget.)

Organization—smooth and logical progression of thought; ideas are presented clearly and effectively; writer uses meaningful transitions (e.g., Also, there is a lot to do at the zoo.)

Development of Ideas/Word Choice—writer develops his/her ideas thoroughly; words chosen are precise and enhance the quality of the writing

Voice—authentic and original voice engages the reader

Conventions/Sentence Fluency—consistent command of spelling, capitalization, punctuation, grammar, usage, and sentence structure skills; ideas are communicated effectively

Unit 4: Expository Writing: Book Report

Score Point 1

I red a book I liked. The book was So many cats. He have so many cats and he dint no what to do. I like swimming to. And runing. His frend took a cat and nother a cat. Then he dint have so many I lik cats too.

Focus and Coherence—lack of focus; weak connection to prompt; purpose of the composition is vague; no sense of completeness

Organization—progression of thought and details are illogical; lacks transitions; ideas are random (e.g., I like swimming to.)

Development of Ideas/Word Choice—very little development of ideas; words may not be used correctly, such as "His frend took a cat and nother a cat."

Voice—individual voice is not expressed in the writing; writer does not engage the reader; lacks connection

Conventions/Sentence Fluency—little to no command of spelling, capitalization, punctuation, grammar, usage, and sentence structure skills; awkward sentences interfere with the ideas communicated by the writer

Score Point 2

My favrite book is Morning On The Farm. It is about a farm. Lots of things happen on farms like roosters and baby cows being born. My mom took us to the beech last year. That was so fun. Farms are fun too. Lots of baby animals live there too. The book has picturs and illustrate. When I read the book I want to visit a farm and see those things. You can read this book!

Focus and Coherence—lacks a strong introduction and conclusion; composition is somewhat focused but includes some extraneous thoughts that do not contribute to the development of the composition, such as "My mom took us to the beech last year."

Organization—writer omits ideas and does not use transitions; ideas are not presented in an effective and logical order

Development of Ideas/Word Choice—writer presents ideas but does not develop them completely; word choice does not suit purpose

Voice—writer engages the reader but fails to sustain the connection; shows little unique perspective

Conventions/Sentence Fluency—limited command of spelling, capitalization, punctuation, grammar, usage, and sentence structure skills; composition is not fluent; sentences are awkward

Score Point 3

My favorite book is Cool Cars, Terrific Trucks. I like this book because it is about cars and trucks. Cars are my favorite thing. I collect toy cars. The book has picturs of many cars and trucks. It gives information about ech car and truck. It tells you how there engines work. Its not too long. This is a good book for somone who wants to know more about cars or trucks. Go read it!

Focus and Coherence—paragraphs and ideas are focused; introduction and conclusion add depth to the composition; sense of completeness

Organization—progression of thought is generally logical; well-organized with a clear beginning, middle, and end; writer presents some unrelated ideas (e.g., I collect toy cars.) but generally stays on topic

Development of Ideas/Word Choice—development of ideas shows depth of thought; writer's word choice suits the composition's purpose but words may be misused, such as *there/their*

Voice—writer uses an authentic and original voice which engages and sustains a connection with the reader

Conventions/Sentence Fluency—good command of spelling, capitalization, punctuation, grammar, usage, and sentence structure skills; writer uses appropriate words and phrases

Score Point 4

If you are looking for a great book to read, I suggest Island of the Wild Ponies. It tells the story of the wild horses that live on the coast of Maryland. The book folows the life of one pony, Athena, from her birth to old age. It dosn't just tell Athena's story but also gives a lot of facts about the wild horses. The photographs and illustrations are beautiful. Island of the Wild Ponies also tells you about the horses' island home and how to get there, in case you want to visit. For a horse lover like me, it was the perfect topic. The book is very fun to read, so pick up a copy today!

Focus and Coherence—composition is focused; writer gives interesting and detailed information about the topic and includes a strong introduction (If you are looking for a great book to read, I suggest Island of the Wild Ponies.) and conclusion (The book is very fun to read, so pick up a copy today!)

Organization—smooth and logical progression of thought; ideas are presented clearly and effectively

Development of Ideas/Word Choice—writer develops his/her ideas thoroughly; words chosen are precise and enhance the quality of the writing

Voice—authentic and original voice engages the reader

Conventions/Sentence Fluency—consistent command of spelling, capitalization, punctuation, grammar, usage, and sentence structure skills; ideas are communicated effectively

Score Point 1

My Class

One time I was in class? One time at scool. I didnt no no one. So it was hard, And it was no fun. I didn't have the rite book to reed. no one lended me one.

I like teecher, She is good. I was afrad to ask for the rite book. but she finly saw and gave to me it. I reeded it. was upsat were over. The end

Focus and Coherence—weak connection to prompt; writer does not give sufficient information about solving a problem at school; purpose of the composition is vague; lacks focus; no sense of completeness

Organization—progression of thought and details are illogical; lacks transitions; ideas are random

Development of Ideas/Word Choice—very little development of ideas; words may not be used correctly, such as "gave to me it"

Voice—individual voice is not expressed in the writing; writer does not engage the reader; lacks connection

Conventions/Sentence Fluency—little to no command of spelling, capitalization, punctuation, grammar, usage, and sentence structure skills; awkward sentences interfere with the ideas communicated by the writer

Unit Assessment

What to Do?

I went to class one morning. It was numbers and art, and I liked the morning work. But then I looked in my back pack. No lunch! I left my lunch at home. So I tryed to think what to do. I was sad with no lunch. I did not want to buther the teacher about it. Then my friend sharred with me. Us each ate half a turky samwich. Peanut butter is my favrit. Someone else gived me a carrit stick. Full now I thanked everyone for helping. That is how I solved my problem.

Focus and Coherence—writer provides information about topic but strays from his/her focus; paragraphs are somewhat focused; superficial introduction and conclusion; composition has some sense of completeness

Organization—ineffective organization; writer includes extraneous details (e.g., Peanut butter is my favrit.); illogical progression of thought; some wordiness and repetition

Development of Ideas/Word Choice—development of ideas is superficial, which limits the reader's understanding of the composition; word choice does not suit purpose (e.g., writer uses "numbers" instead of "Math")

Voice—writer engages the reader but fails to sustain the connection; shows little unique perspective

Conventions/Sentence Fluency— limited command of spelling, capitalization, punctuation, grammar, usage, and sentence structure skills; composition is not fluent; sentences are awkward

Where are They?

I was sick for a week at home. Now I was going back to school. I walked up to my class room and got a big surprise. I didn't know any one there. I didn't know the kids or the teacher. What should I do? Finly I thought up a plan. Insted of going in I would check the other rooms to find my class. I walked in the hall and looked into different rooms. A teacher saw me and asked what I was doing.

" I have bin looking for Ms. Wilson's class."

"Oh I can help."

She led me to the other side of the school. We went in. Their were all my friends. And there was Ms. Wilson too. I found out that Ms Wilson changed rooms with another teacher. I didn't know because I was out for a week. I was very happy to be back.

Focus and Coherence—paragraphs and ideas are focused; introduction and conclusion add depth to the composition; sense of completeness

Organization—progression of thought is generally logical; well-organized

Development of Ideas/Word Choice—development of ideas shows depth of thought; writer uses signal words to show steps taken to resolve the problem

Voice—writer uses an authentic and original voice, which engages and sustains a connection with the reader

Conventions/Sentence Fluency—good command of spelling, capitalization, punctuation, grammar, usage, and sentence structure skills; writer uses appropriate words and phrases

A Bad Day

On Monday, when I got to my classroom, I sat next to my best friend Tia. But something was strange. Tia didn't want to talk to me. I didn't know what to do. Had I done something bad to Tia? I couldn't remembar doing anything meen or bad.

I thought I should stay. That was the only way I would find out what was happening. The best way to fix the problem was to talk to Tia. So that's just what I did. "Tia are you mad at me?"

"No! I am sad is all" Tia said. She did look sad. "We have to find my cat to a new home. Cat fur makes Dad's eyes itch."

"Oh I feel sorry for you!" I said. "Could you come over to my house after school and we could play? My mom knows lots of people who love cats. Maybe someone could help."

"Okay," Tia said. Then she smiled. We were still friends.

Focus and Coherence—composition is focused; writer gives interesting and detailed information about the topic and includes a strong introduction and conclusion

Organization—smooth and logical progression of thought; ideas are presented clearly and effectively

Development of Ideas/Word Choice—writer develops his/her ideas thoroughly; words chosen are precise and enhance the quality of the writing

Voice—authentic and original voice engages the reader

Conventions/Sentence Fluency—consistent command of spelling, capitalization, punctuation, grammar, usage, and sentence structure skills; ideas are communicated effectively

Score Point 1

Games

Crocdils is good. When a kid is off the ground. You can't get them. If their on the ground, then you can, then they are with you.

Cops and robers are all so good. You take a rober to jal. If the rober get out you get them agin, then they trys to get out. Its fun to play crocdils.

Focus and Coherence—writer gives information about two games but does not compare and contrast them; purpose is vague; writing is not coherent

Organization—writing is disorganized; ideas are presented in a random or haphazard way; lacks transitions

Development of Ideas/Word Choice—ideas are not developed; words are omitted and not used correctly (e.g., all so good)

Voice—individual voice is not expressed; composition does not sound authentic or original

Conventions/Sentence Fluency—little to no command of spelling, capitalization, punctuation, grammar, usage, and sentence structure skills; awkward sentences interfere with the ideas communicated by the writer

Fun Games

I like too games. They are simon says and mother may I? Both are fun. Both tells the kids what to do. But the rules are not the same. Card games are fun too.

For the first game kids must hare the words simon says. Than they can move. They take ordurs from Simon. Like Simon could say Put your hands on your head. If he doesn't say his name first, then the player who makes the move is out. They have to be Simon then.

For the other game kids do what mother said. But they have to ask mother may I? If they don't they are out. In the next game. The kid that gets to be mother gives the ordurs. They are both fun games with spechul rules.

Focus and Coherence—writer provides information about two games, but strays from the focus; lacks a strong introduction and conclusion; composition is somewhat focused but includes some extraneous thoughts that do not contribute to the development of the composition

Organization—writer omits ideas and does not use transitions; ideas are not presented in an effective and logical order

Development of Ideas/Word Choice—writer presents ideas but does not develop them completely; word choice does not suit purpose

Voice—writer engages the reader but fails to sustain the connection; shows little unique perspective

Conventions/Sentence Fluency—limited command of spelling, capitalization, punctuation, grammar, usage, and sentence structure skills; composition is not fluent; sentences are awkward

Pirates and Someone Moved

Pirates and Someone Moved are fun to play. They are alike in some ways but not in all. For both, you get into circles. And one player is "it."

The games are not the same. For exampel, the pirate's eyes are covered. Then he sits in the center of the circle. Different key rings go in the middle of the circle. Someone have to crawl up and try to get the keys but not let the pirate hear, if the pirate hears then he gets three turns to point to the one he thinks took keys. If the pirate can't guess, the theef gets to be pirate next.

This is not like what happens in Someone moved. For this game one player moves while "it" is out of the room. Then "it" tries to tell who moved. If he does then that player is "it." So you can see the games are alike and different.

Focus and Coherence—writer compares and contrasts both games; paragraphs and ideas are focused; introduction and conclusion add depth to the composition; sense of completeness

Organization—progression of thought is generally logical; well-organized

Development of Ideas/Word Choice—development of ideas shows depth of thought; writer's word choice suits the composition's purpose

Voice—writer uses an authentic and original voice, which engages and sustains a connection with the reader

Conventions/Sentence Fluency—good command of spelling, capitalization, punctuation, grammar, usage, and sentence structure skills; writer uses appropriate words and phrases

Two Games

Two games I love to play are "hide and seek" and "ghost in the graveyard." These fun games are alike in some ways. Both need at least 3 players. And both are the most fun with a big group. In both games, one or more players hide. Then the other players look for them. The games are the same in one more way. Some of the players try to tag others. You have to be fast to play!

The two games are diferent, too. In hide and seek, all the players but one hide. The player who doesn't hide is "it." But in ghost in the graveyard, only the ghosts hide. Then all the other players look for the ghosts. In hide and seek, "it" must find one of the hidden players. Then "it" tries to tag that player. In the other game, it is the ghosts who try to tag other players. I enjoy playing both games with my friends and the rules are easy to follow.

Focus and Coherence—writer gives interesting, detailed information about two games while comparing and contrasting them

Organization—smooth and logical progression of thought; ideas are presented clearly and effectively; writer uses meaningful transitions

Development of Ideas/Word Choice—writer develops his/her ideas thoroughly; words chosen are precise and enhance the quality of the writing

Voice—authentic and original voice engages the reader

Conventions/Sentence Fluency—consistent command of spelling, capitalization, punctuation, grammar, usage, and sentence structure skills; ideas are communicated effectively

Unit 1 Reteaching and Intervention Opportunities

Tested Skills and Strategies	Teacher's Edition-Small Group	Approaching Reproducibles	Practice Book	ELL Resource Book	Intervention Guide
Comprehension Skills					
Character, 1, 3, 4	33R	5	5	4–11	See Guide
Plot, 2, 6	65R	16	16	16–27	See Guide
Main Idea and Details, 9, 11, 14	77V, 77BB, 77LL, 107X, 107HH	28, 38	28, 38	32–33, 36–45	See Guide
Make/Confirm Predictions, 8	145R, 145X, 145CC	49	49	50–63	See Guide
Vocabulary Strategies					
Word Endings -ed, 5, 10		19, 52	19, 52	50	See Guide
Prefixes, 7, 13		30	30		See Guide
Dictionary/ABC Order, 12		8, 41	8, 41		See Guide
Literary Elements					
Rhyme, 15		21, 43	21, 43		See Guide
Rhythmic Patterns, 16		21, 43	21, 43		See Guide
Text Features and Study Skills					
Photos and Captions, 17		10	10	12, 13, 36, 37	See Guide
Using Parts of a Book, 18		32	32	36	See Guide
Bar Graphs, 19, 20		54	54	65	See Guide
Phonics					
Short o, 25	33L, 33Q, 33W, 33CC, 77O, 107K, 107W, 107CC	2, 11, 44	2, 11, 44		See Guide
Short a, 26	65K, 65Q, 65W, 65X, 65CC, 107W, 107CC, 145L, 145Q, 145W	13, 22, 55	13, 22, 55		See Guide
Short e, 27		13, 22	13, 22		See Guide
Soft c, 28		40, 44	40, 44		See Guide
Consonant Digraph sh, 29		18, 22, 51	18, 22, 51		See Guide
Long o, 30	107W, 107CC, 145L, 145Q, 145W	55	55		See Guide

Language Arts	Grammar Practice Book	TE Unit Writing Process	ELL Practice Book
Grammar, Mechanics, and Usage			
Sentence Capitalization and Punctuation, 21	3, 8		9
Subjects and Predicates, 22	11, 12, 14, 15, 16, 17, 19, 20		14, 19
Sentence Combining, 23	21, 22, 24, 25		24
Letter Punctuation, 24	13		
Phonics			
Short o, 25			1
Short a, 26			6, 21
Short e, 27			6
Soft c, 28			17
Consonant Digraph sh, 29			22
Long o, 30			21
Writing Prompt			
Personal Narrative		151A–151E	

© Macmillan/McGraw-Hill

Unit 2 Reteaching and Intervention Opportunities

Tested Skills and Strategies	Teacher's Edition-Small Group	Approaching Reproducibles	Practice Book	ELL Resource Book	Intervention Guide
Comprehension Skills					
Character, 1, 9	195R, 195X	63	63	70–83	See Guide
Main Idea and Details, 2, 4, 6	247V, 247BB	84	84	108–109	See Guide
Cause and Effect, 3, 11	235R, 235X	74	74	88–103	See Guide
Compare and Contrast, 8	315R, 315X	107	107	130–139	See Guide
Make Inferences, 14	285R, 285X	96	96	112–125	See Guide
Vocabulary Strategies					
Context Clues, 5		60, 65	60, 65		See Guide
Context Clues: Multiple-Meaning Words, 7, 12		76	76		See Guide
Word Parts: Word Families, 10		87	87		See Guide
Word Parts: Suffixes, 13		98, 109	98, 109	114	See Guide
Literary Elements					
Rhyme, 15	285K				See Guide
Rhythmic Patterns, 16					See Guide
Text Features and Study Skills					
Maps, 17		67	67	84	See Guide
Time Lines, 18		111	111	140, 141	See Guide
Photos and Captions, 19		78	78	104, 105, 108, 134	See Guide
Using Parts of a Book, 20		89	89		See Guide
Phonics					
Consonant Blend tr-, 25					See Guide
Consonant Blend dr-, 26		59	59		See Guide
Long a, ay, 27	195K, 195Q, 195W, 195CC				See Guide
Long i, ie, 28	247O, 247P, 247U, 247AA, 247GG	90	90		See Guide
Long o, ow, 29	285K, 285L, 285Q, 285W, 285CC	92, 101	92, 101		See Guide
Long o, oa, 30	285K, 285L, 285Q, 285W, 285CC				See Guide

Language Arts	Grammar Practice Book	TE Unit Writing Process	ELL Practice Book
Grammar, Mechanics, and Usage			
Possessive Nouns, 21	41, 42, 44, 45, 46, 47, 48, 49, 50		44, 49
Proper Nouns, 22	36, 37, 38, 39, 40		39
Using Commas in a Series, 23	28		
Plural Nouns, 24	31, 32, 34, 35, 46, 47, 49, 50		49
Phonics			
Consonant Blend tr-, 25			
Consonant Blend dr-, 26			
Long a, ay, 27			26
Long i, ie, 28			
Long o, ow, 29			41
Long o, oa, 30			
Writing Prompt			
How-to Article		321A–321E	

© Macmillan/McGraw-Hill

Unit 3 Reteaching and Intervention Opportunities

Tested Skills and Strategies	Teacher's Edition- Small Group	Approaching Reproducibles	Practice Book	ELL Resource Book	Intervention Guide
Comprehension Skills					
Summarize, 1, 8, 14	353R, 353X, 387R, 387X, 387HH	119, 131	119, 131	146–155, 160–171	See Guide
Main Idea and Details, 2					See Guide
Author's Purpose, 3, 11	399V, 399BB, 399LL	142	142	176–177	See Guide
Cause and Effect, 4, 6	435R, 435X	152	152	180–191	See Guide
Draw Conclusions, 9	461R, 461X	164	164	196–203	See Guide
Vocabulary Strategies					
Context Clues: Multiple-Meaning Words, 5		144	144		See Guide
Thesaurus, 7, 12		122	122		See Guide
Word Parts: Suffixes, 10		154, 158	154, 158		See Guide
Context Clues, 13	399KK, 435CC, 435GG, 461GG	117, 128, 133, 150, 161	117, 128, 133, 150, 161	149	See Guide
Literary Elements					
Alliteration, 15		124	124	156, 205	See Guide
Onomatopoeia, 16		168	168	204, 205	See Guide
Text Features and Study Skills					
Bar Graphs, 17, 18		157	157	193	See Guide
Choose Research Materials, 19		146	146	193	See Guide
Headings, 20				193, 202	See Guide
Phonics					
Silent Letters -mb, 25		132, 136	132, 136		See Guide
r-Controlled Vowels, 26, 27, 28, 29, 30	353K, 353L, 353Q, 353W, 353CC, 387K, 387Q, 387W, 387CC, 399O, 399P, 399U, 399AA, 399GG, 435K, 435L, 435Q, 435W, 435CC, 461K, 461L, 461W, 461CC	116, 127, 138, 147, 149, 158, 160, 169	116, 127, 138, 147, 149, 158, 160, 169		See Guide

Language Arts	Grammar Practice Book	TE Unit Writing Process	ELL Practice Book
Grammar, Mechanics, and Usage			
Abbreviations, 21	53		
The Verb have, 22	66, 67, 69, 70		69
Past-Tense Verbs, 23	61, 62, 64, 65		64
Book Titles, 24	68		
Phonics			
Silent Letters -mb, 25			57
r-Controlled Vowels, 26, 27, 28, 29, 30			51, 56, 61, 66, 71
Writing Prompt			
Persuasive Letter		467A–467E	

Unit Assessment

Unit 4 Reteaching and Intervention Opportunities

Tested Skills and Strategies	Teacher's Edition-Small Group	Approaching Reproducibles	Practice Book	ELL Resource Book	Intervention Guide
Comprehension Skills					
Sequence of Events, 1, 4, 8	89V, 89BB, 119R, 119X	199, 210	199, 210	244–245, 248–257	See Guide
Author's Purpose, 2					See Guide
Text Structure: Fiction Versus Nonfiction, 3					See Guide
Main Idea and Details, 6					See Guide
Cause and Effect, 9	41R, 41X, 41HH	177	177	210–233	See Guide
Use Illustrations, 13	77R, 77X	188	188	228–239	See Guide
Distinguish Between Fantasy and Reality, 14	161R, 161X	221	221	262–277	See Guide
Vocabulary Strategies					
Word Parts: Compound Words, 5, 12					See Guide
Word Parts: Base Words, 7					See Guide
Dictionary: Homophones, 10		201	201		See Guide
Context Clues, 11	41DD, 41GG, 77DD, 77GG, 89HH, 89KK, 119DD, 119GG, 161DD, 161GG	174, 179, 185, 196, 207	174, 179, 185, 196, 207	213, 249, 264	See Guide
Literary Elements					
Simile, 15		214	214	258	See Guide
Rhyme, 16					See Guide
Text Features and Study Skills					
Drop-Down Menus, 17		181	181	224	See Guide
Floor Plan, 18		192	192	240	See Guide
Using the Internet, 19		203	203	224	See Guide
Written Directions, 20		225	225	241, 278	See Guide
Phonics					
Vowel Diphthong -ow, 25	41K, 41Q, 41W, 41CC	173	173	173	See Guide
Vowel Diphthong -oy, 26	77K, 77L, 77Q, 77W, 77CC	184, 193	184, 193	184, 193	See Guide
Vowel Digraph -oo, 27, 29, 30	89O, 89P, 89U, 89AA, 119K, 119L, 119Q	195, 204, 206, 215	195, 204, 206, 215	195, 204, 206, 215	See Guide
Vowel Digraph -aw, 28	161K, 161Q, 161W, 161CC	217, 226	217, 226	217, 226	See Guide

Language Arts	Grammar Practice Book	TE Unit Writing Process	ELL Practice Book
Grammar, Mechanics, and Usage			
Helping Verbs, 21	81, 82, 84, 85		84
Irregular Verbs, 22	86, 87, 89, 90, 91, 92, 94, 95		89, 94
Quotation Mark, 23	83		
Contractions, 24	96, 97, 98, 99, 100		99
Phonics			
Vowel Diphthong -ow, 25			76
Vowel Diphthong -oy, 26			
Vowel Digraph -oo, 27, 28, 30			
Vowel Digraph -aw, 28			
Writing Prompt			
Expository Writing		167A–167E	

© Macmillan/McGraw-Hill

Unit 5 Reteaching and Intervention Opportunities

Tested Skills and Strategies	Teacher's Edition-Small Group	Approaching Reproducibles	Practice Book	ELL Resource Book	Intervention Guide
Comprehension Skills					
Make Inferences, 1, 3, 6	285R, 285X, 317R, 317X	267, 277	267, 277	320–331, 336–347	See Guide
Sequence of Events, 2, 4, 8	239R, 239X, 239CC, 239HH	244	244	300–311	See Guide
Summarize, 9, 14	251V, 251BB	256	256	316–317	See Guide
Draw Conclusions, 11	205R, 205X	233	233	284–295	See Guide
Vocabulary Strategies					
Context Clues, 5, 13	205DD, 205GG, 239DD, 239GG, 251HH, 251KK, 285DD, 285GG, 317DD, 317GG	231, 236, 242, 253, 275	231, 236, 242, 253, 275	301, 305, 310	See Guide
Word Parts: Base Words, 7, 10					See Guide
Thesaurus, 12		269	269		See Guide
Literary Elements					
Onomatopoeia, 15					See Guide
Rhyme, 16					See Guide
Text Features and Study Skills					
Diagrams and Labels, 17		238	238	296, 297, 313, 333	See Guide
Written Directions, 18		249	249	312	See Guide
Narrow a Topic for Research, 19		260	260		See Guide
Encyclopedia, 20		282	282	346, 347	See Guide
Phonics					
Closed Syllables, 25, 28	205K, 205L, 205Q, 205W, 205CC, 239K, 239L, 239Q, 239W	230, 235, 241, 246, 250	230, 235, 241, 246, 250		See Guide
Open Syllables, 26, 29	251O, 251P, 251U, 251AA, 251GG, 317K, 317L, 317Q, 317W, 317EE	252, 257, 261, 274, 279, 283	252, 257, 261, 274, 279, 283		See Guide
Consonant + le Syllables, 27, 30	285K, 285Q, 285W	263, 268, 272	263, 268, 272		See Guide

Language Arts	Grammar Practice Book	TE Unit Writing Process	ELL Practice Book
Grammar, Mechanics, and Usage			
Quotation Marks, 21	103		
Capitalization, 22	113		
Pronoun I, 23	106, 107, 108, 109, 110		109
Pronoun-Verb Agreement, 24	101, 102, 104, 105, 121, 122, 124, 125		124
Phonics			
Closed Syllables, 25, 28			101, 102, 106, 107
Open Syllables, 26, 29			111, 112, 121, 122
Consonant + le Syllables, 27, 30			116, 117
Writing Prompt			
Realistic Fiction		323A–323E	

© Macmillan/McGraw-Hill

Unit 6 Reteaching and Intervention Opportunities

Tested Skills and Strategies	Teacher's Edition-Small Group	Approaching Reproducibles	Practice Book	ELL Resource Book	Intervention Guide
Comprehension Skills					
Author's Purpose, 1	361R, 361X	291, 308, 330	291, 308, 330	352–363	See Guide
Compare and Contrast, 2, 6	393R, 393X	302	302	368–379	See Guide
Cause and Effect, 3, 8	437R, 437X	323	323	388–399	See Guide
Problem and Solution, 4, 9	405V, 405BB, 461R, 461X	312, 335	312, 335	384–385, 404–411	See Guide
Sequence of Events, 11					See Guide
Fantasy Versus Reality, 14					See Guide
Vocabulary Strategies					
Context Clues: Possessive Nouns, 5		293	293		See Guide
Dictionary: Multiple-Meaning Words, 7		315	315		See Guide
Word Parts: Base Words, 10				371	See Guide
Word Parts: Compound Words, 12		326	326	389	See Guide
Word Parts: Inflectional Nouns, 13					See Guide
Literary Elements					
Repetition, 15		328	328	401	See Guide
Word Choice, 16				400	See Guide
Text Features and Study Skills					
Charts, 17, 18		295	295	364	See Guide
Interview, 19		339	339	413	See Guide
Using Text Features, 20				364	See Guide
Phonics					
r-Controlled Syllables, 25, 30	461K, 461L, 461Q, 461W, 461CC	331, 336, 340	331, 336, 340		See Guide
Vowel Digraph Syllables, 26, 28	393K, 393L, 393Q, 393W, 393CC, 437K, 437L, 437Q, 437W, 437CC	298, 303, 307, 320, 325, 329	298, 303, 307, 320, 325, 329		See Guide
Consonant+le Syllables, 27	361K, 361L, 361Q, 361W, 361CC	287, 292	287, 292		See Guide
Final e Syllables, 29	405O, 405P, 405U, 405AA, 405GG	309, 314, 318	309, 314, 318		See Guide

Language Arts	Grammar Practice Book	TE Unit Writing Process	ELL Practice Book
Grammar, Mechanics, and Usage			
Use the Articles a, an, and the, 21	131, 132, 134, 135		134
Adjectives That Compare, 22	141, 142, 143, 144, 145		144
Adverbs, 23	146, 147, 149, 150		149
Proper Nouns, 24	133		
Phonics			
r-Controlled Syllables, 25, 30			146, 147
Vowel Digraph Syllables, 26, 28			131, 132, 141, 142
Consonant + le Syllables, 27			126, 127
Final e Syllables, 29			136, 137
Writing Prompt			
Compare and Contrast		467A–467E	

Teacher Notes

Teacher Notes

Teacher Notes

© Macmillan/McGraw-Hill

Teacher Notes